Education's Iron Cage

And Its Dismantling In The New Global Order

Bill Anderson
Rita Bouvier
Véronique Brouillette
Raewyn Connell
Nathalie Duceux
Richard Hatcher
Ken Jones
Bruce Karlenzig
Stan Karp
Larry Kuehn
George Martell
Carol Anne Spreen
Salim Vally
Teacher research teams from Korea and Latin America

Our Schools/Our Selves Special Issue
Spring 2006

Our Schools/Our Selves is published four times a year by the Canadian Centre for Policy Alternatives, 410-75 Albert St., Ottawa, ON K1P 5E7. This is Volume 15, Number 3, Issue #83 of the journal (Spring 2006). Our Schools/Our Selves is a member of the Canadian Magazine Publishers Association. It is indexed in the Canadian Magazine Index and the Alternative Press Index.

Executive Editors
Satu Repo and Erika Shaker

Associate Editor
Larry Kuehn

This Issue:
Editor - George Martell
Special thanks to Rita Bouvier, Bob Davis, Richard Hatcher, Larry Kuehn, Loren Lind, Liisa Repo Martell, Grant Sundal

Editorial Office
107 Earl Grey Road, Toronto, ON M4J 3L6, tel or fax (416) 463-6978

Subscriptions and Advertising
Canadian Centre for Policy Alternatives, 410-75 Albert St., Ottawa, ON K1P 5E7, tel: (613) 563-1341 fax: (613) 233-1458

ISSN 0840-7339
ISBN 0-88627-474-5

Production
Typesetting and design: Nancy Reid. Printed in Canada by Imprimerie Gagne, 80 Ave. St. Martin, Louiseville, PQ J5V 1B4. Publications Mail Registration No. 8010.

Cover Design
Nancy Reid - www.nrgrafix.com

Front Cover Photo Illustration
Dirk van Stralen - www3.telus.net/vanstralen/

Contents

Introduction: Education's Iron Cage And Its Dismantling In The New Global Order

GEORGE MARTELL

At the core of this book is an understanding that what we love in the world – what we struggle to achieve in our schools (as in our lives) – comes first, not just as an ethical imperative, but first historically.

This should be an obvious starting point in setting out to understand the global experience of public schooling. But it is not. It is, in fact, a reality we often forget as we react to the inhumanity we experience of the world's educational systems, especially if we are among the world's working peoples/colonized peoples. In the everyday life of our schools, a subordinate-class impetus to build a just and caring educational system often appears more as an impulsive *reaction* to an offensive and overwhelming framework of ruling-class policies and practices; it doesn't seem to have an identity or a life of its own. What we have to keep in mind is that in the bigger pattern of educational change, this subordinate-class impetus, in fact, comes first and the thrust of our ruling class in education comes later. Ruling-class action in public education is primarily a response to an ongoing popular demand for schools that genuinely enhance the lives of their students; it reflects the need of those in power to restrain and reshape a fundamental human desire to build a better future for their children.

This understanding is often implicit rather than explicit in these pages, but it serves as bedrock for any future action we may take in resisting the current neo-liberal assault on our public schools. The iron cage of global capitalism, now pressing heavily on the world's schools, should be seen as an aggressive ruling-class *reaction* to a continuous subordinate-class insistence on building a world for themselves and on exploring the knowledge necessary for such a task. Feudal peasants, First Nations communities, artisans and small farmers, industrial workers of all countries, and the peasantry of globalized "underdevelopment" have all fought for such a world and have all contributed to the knowledge needed to build it in the future. This struggle, reflected in the articles that follow, continues around the globe, and the knowledge it contains is there for us, however repressive our current circumstances may be.

In the present day, what has developed as the dominant form of global education has emerged out of the growing strength of international capital in suppressing post-war worker militancy and national liberation. The focus of this form of education is on deepening corporate control of the world's working people. At the same time, however, because capital does not command all power, its educational structures still have to take into account the immediate demands of these subordinate classes (for their own world and the knowledge to build it). Capital also has to recognize the prospect that subordinate-class power will eventually grow in opposition once more and that earlier institutional "forms of hope" (in education as elsewhere) will eventually be reconstituted and reshaped in the struggle for a new world. Most of these immediate demands are, of course, actively resisted by those in power. Some are co-opted and some find their way into actually implemented policy. Potential subordinate-class power, on the other hand, finds its way into the policy process through the back door of governing-class prudence. The end product in the real world of our school systems is sometimes called an "education settlement" – a resultant or compromise of forces (primarily class forces) held in place for a significant moment in time, but always (potentially) unstable, as these forces are continually on the move and shifting in relative strength. If the papers in this book are any indication, we may be at the beginning of another shift in these forces and the growth of subordinate-class power in our schools. Or we may not. A new resistance movement in our schools appears to be in the making, but we have yet no clear grasp on its eventual outcome.

What *is* evident – as our authors attest – is the continuing strength of capitalism's assault on public schooling over the last three decades or so in both its neo-conservative and its neo-liberal variants.

The central purposes of this assault are also clear: First, to increase capitalist profits through financial cutbacks (allowing tax cuts for the rich and the corporations) and through outsourcing school services (expanding the school marketplace for private profit); this process is often called "privatization." The second purpose of this assault is to intensify the production of human capital in the schools, especially low-level human capital among children who are poor, immigrant or migrant, and who come from communities of colour. Capitalism requires increasing numbers of workers, citizens and consumers who willingly do what they are told to do and think what they are told to think. The production of such human capital is the most fundamental role schools play in capitalist society.

But while its strength is obvious and its overall aims are clear, the on-the-ground nature of this assault is still hard to pin down.

Global capitalism has hit schools around the world with such force and speed that those who stand in opposition have yet to recover enough space to really take in what has happened. Furthermore, the assault in still coming in new manipulative language and within ever-changing frameworks of curriculum delivery and bureaucratic and technical control. Simply bringing us up-to-date in a number of key areas takes up a major part of this collection.

THE PRIVATIZATION AGENDA

An equally important reason for our inability to deal with this assault as clearly as we might is the intensity of its privatization thrust. This thrust has been so destructive of public education that it has taken up most of the time and energy of progressive forces in our schools. Our thinking about the larger purposes of schooling has been buried in a struggle in which public education itself seemed to be on the line. As a result, the human capital side of the current corporate agenda in education has yet to be resisted in any substantial way. School-based human capital production has, of course, been widely criticized for its human emptiness and social divisiveness. In particular, the curriculum core of this production – Outcomes (or Expectations) Based Education (OBE) policed by standardized tests – has faced growing opposition, particularly among teachers. This opposition, however, has yet to take on serious organizational strength. In large part, as the articles in this book make clear, this is because the intensity of the privatization thrust has not diminished.

For all the official corporate humanism that opened the 21st century, with its emphasis on building "social cohesion" in an increasingly unruly world, very little of this emphasis has reached the ground of actual practice – at least in terms of social democratic manoeuvring. New Right conservatism has largely been replaced by New Right liberalism, which has focused on intensifying and rationalizing earlier conservative institutions and reforms. The overall direction of public policy has remained solidly in place over the last three decades. Raw corporate power — and the pressure for immediate profit-making opportunities — is still very much in evidence in government decision-making circles. It continues to trump more long-term capitalist concerns for social cohesion and more humane human capital development.

As a result, the privatization of public schooling in all its forms continues around the globe.

Governments have hung tough on tax relief for the rich and the corporations. They have kept the neo-conservative financial structures in place that demanded extensive social-service cutbacks to ensure this tax relief. This has been especially the case in countries with rising military, police, court and jail costs. Occasionally, in jurisdictions where school funding has become a hot-button political issue, a little more money has gone to education at the expense of other social sectors. But relative to what our school systems need, the new funds are a drop in the bucket; they don't come anywhere close to dealing with such fundamentals as the backlog in school building and repair and the continuing downward pressure on teacher and education-worker salaries. In many countries, there is a continuing decline in real per pupil spending. It is also worth noting that much of the limited new money is disappearing into targeted projects – like implementing and policing the new Outcomes Based Education curriculum and testing policies – that hurt rather than help the public system.

Outsourcing to the private sector is also growing, bringing with it an additional for-profit financial squeeze on the public schools.

More public money continues to flow into private schooling, with elite schools and religious schools taking most of it. With this money –

and in response to the continuing assault on public education – private schooling continues to expand.

In all of the countries we have examined, there is also continuing extension of the private sector within public education.

A growing number of for-profit activities are going on inside our public school systems. They include teacher training, curriculum development (from literacy programs to technical education), lesson plan packaging, consulting on policy development, setting up education business sectors for international competition, school bus programs, cleaning services, repair services, secretarial services, food services, publishing ventures, school management, graphic design, payroll distribution, program sponsorship, voucher development, supplemental tutoring, and last, but not least, the construction and maintenance of public schools to be owned by private companies for various lengths of time and rented back (at a fat profit) to governments and local authorities. We have whole sections of school bureaucracies dedicated to opening up "public-private partnerships."

There is also a growing number of what might be described as non-profit, pro-business activities going on inside the public schools.

There is increasing pressure to make public education function more like a private corporation. School systems are now led by CEOs and hierarchies of "managers" promoting various forms of competition between local authorities, local schools, teachers and students as well as a variety of standardized measurements to determine the winners and the losers in this competition. Increasingly, the task of school authorities is the protection and development of an internal competitive marketplace and the deepening of social class divisions. "Successful" public schools are encouraged to recruit a middle-class clientele while increasing numbers of poor children are obliged to find their way into poor schools and bottom streams, which are stripped of even more resources when they fail to achieve middle-class "standards." Middle-class parents are pressed to help fund what amounts to their own private schools within the public system and to distance themselves from the system's lower-class failures. Teachers of poor children, on the other hand, are pressed to make up the difference for their students out of their own pockets. Vouchers and charter schools are another part of this complex mix. There is also growing pressure to bring competitively minded business and religious ideologues directly into school management, with England and America leading the way. As in the capitalist world outside the school, in these new "competitive" structures educational policies and resources are skewed in the direction of the well to do.

THE IRON CAGE

For all the power of its impact – and the growth in profits it entails – the privatization thrust of neo-liberal education contains real dangers for the future of capitalist society. In many respects, it runs against the grain of human capital production, robbing the educational system of the resources necessary to implement an effective human capital policy.

This is a genuine problem for capitalism. The dramatic need for short-term profits appears to be undercutting the requirement for long-term social control as a basis for long-term profit. As a result – as more thoughtful members of capitalism's governing classes have predicted – the "social cohesion" of our societies has become more fragile. In the education sector, working people can now plainly see that their local schools are crumbling, not just in their physical plant and in the resources available to them, but in officials' ability to defend their practices with both students and parents. What has become especially evident is that these local schools are promoting much deeper social divisions. Nowhere is this clearer than in poor immigrant communities of colour.

It may be a moment when the issue of human capital production (particularly its low-level variety) can again come to the surface in our schools. It is no longer hidden as it once was in the efficient functioning of what Loren Lind called "the learning machine."

But those who put this human capital issue forward – who struggle for purpose and meaning in our schools – will still have to contend with what Bouvier and Karlenzig later in this book refer to as the "iron cage [of] functional rationality and instrumentality" that the capitalist order has created over the centuries in its quest for a stable marketplace for goods and labour.

This iron cage is not a "sheath of steel" as Weber originally imagined it before the term was translated for an English-speaking audience. It is more open and more vulnerable to attack. It takes different forms in different institutions and in different societies. It can be sophisticated or roughly cast. It is, nevertheless, a structure of great power in whatever form it takes.

The term "iron cage" can be applied across whole societies in describing a structure of coercive economic and psychological relationships whose central function is the creation of human capital. This is human capital production broadly understood as the creation of workers and citizens and consumers, who bring together in their own persons that uniquely capitalist fusion of intellectual passivity and energetic action. It is perhaps best understood as a process of standardization, which as much as possible hopes to make people like machines or, at least, effective extensions of machines.

The standardization process itself can be divided into two thoroughly integrated parts. The first part is a two-sided *control thrust*: it moves to cut people off from their human ties and from the natural world (undercutting solidarity, encouraging objectification) while it pressures them, at the same time, to accept their individual place (and sometimes their communal place) within a complex social hierarchy and to take orders from those above them in authority. The second part is the *standardized action* that is to emerge out of this control thrust: action that supports capitalist profit in the workplace, in the marketplace and in the state system. The capacity and willingness to take such action in all these areas is the central meaning of human capital.

The current form of such standardized action emerged with the development of "scientific management" at the end of the nineteenth century and the rise of "industrial psychology," which followed. Together these two developments created a particularly modern combination of economic coercion and psychological manipulation in response to working-class unrest.

We might think of the entire process as an aggressive extension of economic rationality to all social domains.

Such an iron cage increasingly forms the core governance and curriculum structure of our schools. Outcomes Based Education is its most recent expression. It contains and links the *control thrust* for turning students into human capital and the *standardized action* that is the most practical expression of this human capital. OBE separates students and teachers from society and nature, while encouraging acquiescence and obedience to those in authority. At the same time, it directs students and teachers into learning the increasingly dissociated (and demeaning) hard and soft "skills" that capitalism requires of us.

As our contributors show us, OBE has spread across the world in company with the economic, political and military might of global capitalism and western imperialism. Resistance to OBE will grow as the resistance to global capitalism and western imperialism grows.

DISMANTLING THE IRON CAGE

From capitalism's perspective, the dismantling of public education – particularly its physical and human framework – is thoroughly underway.

It is a process, as I've indicated, that has had unintended consequences.

Public school systems are actually disintegrating. This is what happens to an iron cage – if I can stretch the metaphor – when it's neglected or left out in the rain. It rusts. It falls apart. It loses its authority and its holding power.

The privatization agenda of cutbacks and outsourcing has hammered the material and personnel basis of our public school systems and continues to do so. As a result, their authority and power among working people have been slipping away.

For all the destruction caused by privatization, it creates an opportunity for more deep-rooted political organizing – at the local school level and at all other levels of government that determine education policy.

It is an opportunity that lets us expand the struggle not only for more money in our schools, but also for a much more democratic education and for a challenging curriculum that genuinely opens students and teachers to the physical, social and spiritual world around them.

As this collection shows, there are a number of steps being taken to move us in all three of these directions.

In the process, of course, we are in direct opposition to the neo-liberal thrust of the corporate world. We are engaged in dismantling the iron cage of capitalist control and skill development in education. We are also involved in restoring the resources capitalism has taken from our schools.

What I want to offer here is a rough summary of where global resistance to neo-liberalism (in both its conservative and liberal forms) has been leading us. It is a set of conclusions that emerge, it seems to me, from the essays that follow.

Wherever we are, it turns out, the big problem is keeping things together: building coalitions and centering them on working-class and peasant organizing in alliance with the work being done by Indigenous communities; keeping the issues of money, power and curriculum interlocked; and linking our demands for what should be abandoned in our school systems with what should be put in its place.

Working together

There is no getting around the need for powerful coalitions in education. Students, teachers, education workers, parents, communities, and the labour movement all have to be together on this front. If they're split – as they are far too often these days – we're doomed. Every sympathetic organization available has to be organized on this front – to establish a common position and fight for it together.

This organizing can't just be reactive to the neo-liberal assault on our schools. Underneath it there has to be a vision of a just and caring society that schooling helps build as well as a grasp of the knowledge and wisdom needed to build it.

Our organizing has to reach out on two fronts simultaneously: It has to impact the political institutions that make overall decisions about public schooling (within national, regional, and local governments) and it has to be rooted in local schools (where core organizing has to take place and where real changes can be made, sometimes in direct opposition to centralized ministries of education). What's required are tough political structures – with forms as various as urban education political parties, regional education networks and sections of national political organizations – that can deliver electoral votes where needed and can also function as an organizing framework and social movement within the public schools. These structures have to provide overall leadership and vision in the struggle for genuine knowledge, which reconnects us to "people and place" and to larger social purposes across our educational systems. At the same time, this leadership must press hard for the democratization of curriculum, pedagogy and governance in neighbourhood schools

The organizing also has to have a working-class and/or a peasant base as well as roots in Indigenous communities. While as many progressive middle-class parents and activists as possible have to be integrated into the organization, if it isn't focused primarily on improving the situation of working-class, peasant and aboriginal children it will die, and public schooling will continue to get beaten up. Public-sector teacher unions especially have to grasp this reality. Workers, peasants and Aboriginal peoples need a public system, and they will defend it – if it answers their needs. The middle class, however, as has been evident over the last couple of decades, can be seduced or pushed out of the public schools; its members increasingly chose private schooling as a solution to public sector woes. Special care therefore has to be taken to ensure that teacher interests and working-class, peasant and Aboriginal peoples interests are solidly linked in certain key demands: smaller classes linked to de-streaming; teacher freedom to do honest work (including the right to run their own profession) that results in a more challenging and meaningful curriculum; parental engagement that makes a difference in discipline and shared purpose; better wages and working conditions for teachers and education workers that not only leads to happier classrooms but also to a broader pattern of upward wage gains for all. Finally, it is worth noting that the building of stronger schools in this fashion will have the effect of drawing back disaffected middle-class parents, who have left for the private sector but still believe in a public system.

Money, power, curriculum

Just as all the progressive players in education have to be brought together in coalitions, the three basic issues of money, power and curriculum (including pedagogy and assessment) have to be brought together into one platform.

It is increasingly important not to focus on one issue to the detriment of the others, as we have done so much of late in privileging the financial problems our school systems face. These three issues have to be integrated in organizing educational reform. When we say we need more money, we also have to say how it will be spent and where it will be spent. When we support a particular approach to curriculum, we also have to describe how it will be funded and what kind of democracy is involved both in the classroom and in the school as a whole. When we demand a particular form of governance, we have to lay out what that will mean for the ways we make decisions about money or the development and implementation of program.

Keeping these three areas together is not only fundamental to putting forward a vision of an alternative school system, it is also strategically essential, if we are to keep our coalitions intact. We need this complete picture in front of us (supported by all its contributors) if we are, for example, to prevent teachers from walking away from curriculum issues, once their pay and working conditions are settled, or if we are stop parent neglect of teacher and education-worker wages in order to focus on issues of program and parent power. Parents have to hang tough politically on the wages and working conditions front and teachers have to demand curriculum and governance reforms in their contracts.

Democratic process and program priorities are particularly important in working out alternative budgets. We have to put real options for revenue and spending in front of people – options from minimum tax increases on the rich and the corporations to fund current shortfalls to a much more thorough grounding of the public accounts (including those of education) to assure long-term revenue sources and to set out long-term spending priorities.

Saying No and saying Yes

We have to learn to say No to policies and programs we don't want and Yes to those we do want – at the same time.

We have to say No to human capital production in our schools as we say Yes to a program that fits all our students for the task of building a genuine home for themselves in communities and countries they can call their own.

We have to put a stop to the "abstraction" of academic knowledge and work instead to help students put together thought and action in their curriculum (in everything from working to improve neighbourhood life to taking on environmental issues).

We have to stand opposed to all versions of Outcomes Based Education while we build a program that honestly explores and grapples with the reality in which we are centred. This means unequivocal resistance to an imposed framework of one-dimensional outcomes as well as broad support for open-ended areas of exploration, collectively developed, that permit teachers and students to move into purposeful work together.

This opposition extends to all forms of standardized tests and looks instead to what is often called "authentic assessment," which allows students to show or give expression to what they know and allows teachers to continuously move them forward. It means we reject academic competition while we collectively support the highest quality work from all our students.

We also have to stand against all forms of socially biased labels – class- race- culture- and gender-biased – and insist that all students are treated as full human beings in relationship with one another, with histories and stories yet to be told.

At the same time, we have to reject socially biased forms of streaming or tracking and demand a "comprehensive" de-streamed system that provides the resources to ensure that all students get a "quality" education.

We have to be clear that human capital production in worker training is not acceptable at the same time as we insist on solid technical education that incorporates a strong Arts and Science program – its courses equally sophisticated to those of any university-bound program and recognized as such. We have to resist education's role in craft deskilling while we move technical studies in the direction of science, as all serious craftwork has traditionally moved.

We have to oppose the separation of mental and manual work while we struggle for programs that allow all students to experience both. We have to protest the mindless acceptance of capitalism's mode of production while we support a much deeper understanding of the larger social, economic, and industrial design structures of our students' future workplaces.

We have to say No to under-funding, as we have said for many years now, and Yes to a genuine base for stable and generous school finance.

We have to say No to huge educational institutions and Yes to small local authorities (or boards), small schools and small classes.

We have to challenge a top-down corporate governance structure and demand democratic governance that takes into account the need for common aims and resource allocation, but at the same time encourages and supports a thorough-going democratization of local schools. We have to stand against the centralized coercion and manipulation that currently oppresses our schools while we support the creation of effective models of school reform – models that may apply to large jurisdictions but which allow local schools to choose what they want and to create what they need.

We have to resist the "teacher-proofing" of our schools (including destructive teacher assessment procedures) while fighting for a structure that lets our teachers teach.

We have to oppose the mindless hierarchy in which school board workers do their jobs and organize for their complete integration into the work of the school and its decision-making process.

Finally, we must say No to a corporate-controlled agenda that denies the character of the child and disrespects community while we say Yes to an extensive mobilization of teacher, student, parent and community knowledge that can genuinely strengthen children's lives.

The contributors to this collection do not imagine this alternative program will find major traction any time soon.

But we know that without such a broad program in front of us – shaped to our particular circumstances and guiding our action – our immediate work for more limited changes in our schools can never come to fruition. What we do now has to link with a clear understanding of what our future school systems can become. Without that direction, our current politics of educational reform will inevitably be co-opted and undercut by those who currently have power in our schools.

As Claudia Korol, an Argentinian journalist, put it recently: "Believe what is necessary is possible. Accomplish what is possible."

Accountability and Aboriginal Education: Dilemmas, Promises and Challenges

RITA BOUVIER AND BRUCE KARLENZIG

INTRODUCTION

Ten years ago, in her introduction to a collection of essays in which various contributors focused on the state of First Nations education, Marie Battiste (1995: xiv) identified the following questions that Aboriginal communities faced when assuming control of their schools:

What goals and outcomes are important? What processes must accompany cultural and linguistic development and inclusion? What is the meaning of renewal and revision in the contemporary and traditional educational context? How do we represent our cultures in schools? Should we teach and evaluate in traditional Aboriginal ways or adopt contemporary Eurocentric models of education to achieve a diversity of goals?

A decade later, these questions continue to have relevance for parents, educators and political leaders, and not only for Aboriginal persons. Indigenous knowledge and ways of teaching and learning offer a wealth of interesting possibilities and benefits for all individuals – Aboriginal and non-Aboriginal – and communities (Battiste, 2000: 202). Unfortunately, for various reasons non-First Nations, Métis or Inuit governments within Canada have tended to resist acting upon this insight. Moreover, in recent years attempts to implement culturally affirming and sustainable Aboriginal education opportunities within publicly funded, pre-K-12 provincial education systems have been further complicated by demands for more "accountability," particularly through an increased emphasis on the measurement of students' academic achievement outcomes.

THE CASE OF SASKATCHEWAN

Saskatchewan's provincial education system represents an interesting example through which to consider how this understanding of accountability presents some important dilemmas, promises, and challenges for Aboriginal education. Compared to other provinces, a relatively high proportion of Saskatchewan's population is Aboriginal (13.5% according to the 2001 census). This proportion is growing, although recently the trend has been slowing down somewhat (Saskatchewan Learning, 2004b: 6-7). In addition, the median age (20.1 years) of Aboriginal persons in Saskatchewan is younger than in any other province. Approximately 20% of the province's school-aged population is Aboriginal (Saskatchewan Learning, 2004b: 109).[1] While a high proportion (82%) of First Nations students living on-reserve attend First Nations schools,[2] most First Nations students living off-reserve as well as Métis students in Saskatchewan are enrolled in the provincial system.

Aboriginal Education and Indigenous Knowledge

A persistent legacy of the colonization of Aboriginal peoples is that "Canada and its provincial curricula have continued to marginalize or be indifferent to First Nations peoples" as well as the educational aspirations of Inuit and Métis societies, respectively (Smith, 2001: 77; Canadian Council on Learning, 2005: 6-9; B.C. Teachers' Federation, 2002: 30). Even where efforts to introduce Aboriginal education have taken hold, provincial education systems and institutions have developed somewhat different ideas about what this concept means and how this education should be offered. In some cases, for example, a system or institution has taken an additive approach (some might call it tokenism) in which distinct subjects or courses about Aboriginal issues (e.g., "Native Studies") have been inserted into an already established and basically Eurocentric curriculum (Robertson, 2003: 552). In other cases, limited Aboriginal content or perspectives may have been grafted onto one or more pre-existing courses (e.g., humanities courses, the natural or social sciences, and so on).

An alternative is to take a much more holistic position by recognizing that, rather than simply being an "add on" to the more familiar curricula and pedagogies, Aboriginal education can involve a qualitatively different and transformative process for teaching and learning. This process embraces Indigenous peoples' worldviews, social structures, and pedagogy as a legitimate foundation upon which to construct new meanings or knowledge alongside Western traditions and ways of knowing.

From this point of view, Aboriginal education is understood to be grounded in Indigenous knowledge, comprehensive and distinct knowledge systems with their own "epistemology, philosophy, and scientific and logical validity" (Daes as cited in Battiste and Henderson, 2000: 41). Like other contemporary knowledge systems, Indigenous knowledge is not an abstraction or historical artifact; rather, it is a lived experience on the part of individuals and communities who, through shared languages and ongoing social relations, continually construct, maintain, and modify their understandings of who they are and what they know (Battiste, 1998: 18; Battiste and Henderson, 2000: 49-52).

Key elements of Indigenous knowledge include a focus on relationships, patterns, and processes, particularly the interconnections and inter-dependence among all living beings (including human beings) and places.[3] Infused within all aspects of reality is a power or living energy that is experienced as personal, situated in place (relationships), and because of its moral dimension, sacred. With its attention to the wholeness and sacred qualities within all beings and places, Indigenous knowledge stands in marked contrast to most Western dichotomies (e.g, objectivity vs. subjectivity, the "natural world" vs. the "human world" and so on). All aspects of reality, including Indigenous knowledge itself, are assumed to be communal and shared, and involve both an individual and community responsibility to maintain reciprocal relationships and the balance or harmony that is essential to all life (Battiste and Henderson, 2000: 42-43; Smith, 2001: 80).

Indigenous knowledge sees awareness of oneself as the beginning of learning. The unexplained is respected as the great mystery and wisdom is understood to come from direct experience and reflection (Erasmus, 2002: 1; Hébert, 2000: 71). In the context of education, what is perhaps most significant is the belief that the common good is centered not on human society alone, but on the natural environment that forms one's political and ethical community. The basic question for all learners is "How does what I have learned affect our relations (place) and existence?"

Saskatchewan's Aboriginal Education Policy

Through the years, the provincial government in consultation with various partner organizations as well as First Nations and Métis spokespersons has developed a number of policy statements that focus on Aboriginal education. The central policy (initially adopted in 1989) takes the following position:

[The Department of Learning] recognizes that the [Aboriginal] peoples of the province are historically unique peoples occupying a unique and rightful place in society. [The Department of Learning] recognizes that education programs must meet the needs of [Aboriginal] students, and that changes to existing programs are also necessary for the benefit of *all students*. (Saskatchewan Learning, 1989: 6. Emphasis added.)

This policy as well as the development of education programs and services that may result are guided by four key principles:

1) [Aboriginal] peoples have the opportunity to participate fully in the planning, design and delivery and, where applicable, co-management of the education system at all levels.
2) The education system recognizes [Aboriginal] students are the children of peoples whose cultures are, in many ways, different from those who established the school system. These differences which may include learning styles, language and worldview, must be reflected in curriculum, programs, teaching methods and climate in the schools attended by [Aboriginal] children.
3) There is a coordination of efforts to meet the needs of [Aboriginal] students in the communities in which they live. There is ongoing consultation and cooperation between and among federal and provincial governments and their agencies, local education and community development authorities.

4) Programs to improve the success of [Aboriginal] students in school are focused primarily at the school community level. (Saskatchewan Learning, 1989: 5).[4]

Through the years, a number of related policies have also been developed, especially with regard to community schools, Aborginal languages, special education, and equity in education. Recognizing that, although some valuable progress had been made through the implementation of these policies, the educational needs of First Nations and Métis students in the provincial system had still not been realized, the government released a complementary policy framework in 2003 ("Building Partnerships: First Nations and Métis People in the Provincial Education System". See Saskatchewan Learning, 2003.) This framework was developed through the involvement of various representatives and other individuals throughout the educational community, including officials from the Federation of Saskatchewan Indian Nations (FSIN) and the Métis Nation of Saskatchewan (MNS). It includes five basic goals:

- improved supports and educational outcomes for First Nations and Métis students;
- shared management and governance in the provincial education system;
- high quality learning programs for *all students*. (Emphasis added. Part of this goal is to ensure that "Aboriginal content and perspectives [should be] integral to all subject areas so that all children and youth gain knowledge, insight and understanding".]
- compatible and transferable practices and reciprocal relationships between provincial and First Nations schools;
- a shared and harmonious future. (Saskatchewan Learning, 2003: 4-5.)

This framework also refers to a continuum of partnership agreements and shared responsibilities among the provincial education system and First Nations and Métis authorities that either already exist or could readily be established in the province including cooperative partnerships, co-management partnerships and co-governance partnerships. These partnerships as well as the overall policy framework respect the Aboriginal and Treaty rights of the Aboriginal peoples of Canada.

Implementation of Aboriginal Education Policies

On a provincial level, implementation of the policies and framework has been uneven. Much has been accomplished in the form of partnership agreements, curriculum renewal with a focus on Indigenous knowledge and perspectives, a major expansion of the Community Schools program (including a pre-kindergarten program), the development of many learning resources pertaining to Aboriginal education, the ongoing success of highly innovative Aboriginal Teacher Education Programs, the introduction of various instructional strategies and learning opportunities at the local level, the establishment or expansion of programs and program supports (e.g., an Aboriginal Elder/Outreach program), and the facilitation of numerous professional development opportunities for teachers and non-teaching school staff members (Saskatchewan Learning, 2004a: 7-10).

Less progress has been evident, however, in overcoming the long-standing racism and systemic barriers that many Aboriginal students experience and which significantly limit their academic achievement, social acceptance, and overall success in schools (St. Denis et. al., 1998: 53-56; St. Denis and Hampton, 2002: 8-10; Battiste and McLean, 2005: 2-3; Hodgson-Smith, 2005: 17). Some teachers also have a professional development need to improve their understanding about Aboriginal education generally, as well as to acquire a greater range of pedagogical skills that would affirm Aboriginal ways of knowing, teaching, and learning (Saskatchewan Learning, 2004b: 110; Hodgson-Smith, 2005: 19; Wotherspoon, 2004: 17).

Layered into this provincial context for Aboriginal education has been an approach to educational accountability that for the most part has carefully avoided the relentless zeal for standardized testing of students, ranking and rating of schools, and teacher testing that has plagued education systems elsewhere in Canada or in states south of the border. Saskatchewan has participated in some national and international student achievement testing programs, but not to the detriment of provincial or local student assessment and evaluation programs or processes.

At least, not so far. Recently, however, government officials have signalled their disappointment with Saskatchewan students' results on the tests associated with the School Achievement Indicators Program (SAIP) and the Programme for International Student Assessment (PISA). The government has announced a new set of "Three 'Rs'" (responsiveness, relevance, and results) that are intended to make the education system more accountable, especially by directing more attention to instruction and student outcomes in subject areas that are associated with post-secondary entrance requirements, transition-to-work skills, and perceived labour market needs.[5]

TWO STEPS FORWARD, THREE STEPS BACK: KEY DILEMMAS AND CONTRADICTIONS OF ACCOUNTABILITY AND ABORIGINAL EDUCATION

The Saskatchewan government's strategy is aimed at "solving" an apparent cluster of socio-economic problems. Too many students, especially off-reserve First Nations and Métis students, are not achieving at acceptable levels in subjects such as math and the sciences. Too many of these students are leaving school before completion of grade 12. Too many of these students fail to obtain gainful employment. And too many job openings, particularly in the skilled trades, will go unfilled in the future as the baby boom generation retires, leading to major difficulties in the economy.

By taking steps to make the provincial education system more accountable and by promoting the "new Three 'Rs'", the government hopes to "engage" all students in schools (if not in their education), improve the province's national and international standings regarding student achievement scores, and deal with a supposedly looming labour shortage by funnelling students, especially Aboriginal students it would seem, into certain types of employment.

The globalization context

The Saskatchewan government's approach to accountability appears to be evolving in ways that are consistent with what has already taken place in other provinces or countries. As documented extensively in the research literature, this kind of push for ever-more accountability in education may be understood as a manifestation of much broader globalization developments that involve the privatization, deregulation, and de-professionalization of the welfare state and the incremental commodification of publicly funded education (Froese-Germain, 2005: 57; Canadian Teachers' Federation, 2004: 4-10; Kohn, 2000: 3; Sacks, 1999: 68-93).

Part of the problem is that accountability is becoming defined in fairly narrow terms that may be appropriate in a business setting (e.g., performance or achievement scores, "client" satisfaction, the ranking of institutions), but are not congruent with the goals and values of a complex public sector service that, on the surface at least, is supposed to meet highly diverse educational responsibilities and community expectations, respect and affirm students' cultures, respond to the unique qualities and needs of individual students, and nurture each student's growth as a whole person. Moreover, publicly funded education is supposed to be a shared responsibility in which students, parents, teachers, administrators, elected officials, and entire communities recognize that they each must do their part to create an educational environment that is conducive to teaching and learning. This principle of shared responsibility should be accompanied by a commitment to shared accountability, broadly defined. Unfortunately, that commitment is typically overlooked by proponents of the so called "accountability revolution" that is now well underway in Canada, the United States, and elsewhere. In this revolution, it would appear that the only people, other than students, who actually seem to be held accountable are teachers.

DILEMMAS AND CONTRADICTIONS

The implications of these developments for Aboriginal education in Saskatchewan are multi-faceted and may be instructive for educators in other provinces. Our view is that accountability within a publicly funded education system is always necessary, but a reductionist approach that equates accountability with tougher student performance benchmarks, standardized test results, and student outcomes is fraught with too many dilemmas and contradictions to benefit Aboriginal education (at least insofar as how this concept has been articulated earlier in this paper).

A fundamental difficulty is that the assumptions and biases that are typically integral to these accountability models (e.g., a worldview that reflects the values and beliefs of the dominant culture, an ethic of competitiveness, a standardized definition and operationalization of students' "success" or "progress", the ranking and rating of individuals and social institutions, a fragmented and technical approach to teaching and learning, etc.) are not congruent with Indigenous knowledge or the norms and values of many Aboriginal cultures. As noted by Melnechenko and Horsman (1998: 7), for example, "success in one culture may not be defined the same as it is in another. It is the different people involved in the students' education who have different views of success that constitutes its meaning. Aboriginal communities often define success as mastering a curriculum and retaining cultural heritage. A European culture measures success in school by measuring academic achievement."

Other dilemmas and contradictions that technical-managerial (Biesta, 2004: 234)[6] or "outcomes" accountability models pose for Aboriginal education include the following:

1. At the same time that many educators and parents have expressed growing concerns about the educational merits of the "accountability revolution" that has taken hold in a number of Canadian jurisdictions, Aboriginal education (and the comparisons between Aboriginal and non-Aboriginal students regarding academic achievement levels) is being used to justify the implementation of more outcomes-based models of accountability. The main rationale for the public policy commitment to this view of accountability[7] is that supposedly the achievement levels of Aboriginal students will improve over time, thereby enabling more individuals to make successful transitions to post-secondary programs and/or the workforce.

   Two implications of this rationale are especially problematic. The first is that there seems to be an assumption that progress in socio-economic status and equity within a society are mainly, if not solely, a result of improved achievement scores.

What this perspective minimizes or even overlooks (some might say intentionally) are the kinds of systemic factors that have constructed and perpetuated existing inequities (Kohn, 2000: 38-40). In the context of Aboriginal education, a key factor has been the historical marginalization of Indigenous peoples' knowledge, histories, and experiences.

The second implication of the rationale for a greater emphasis on academic achievement results or outcomes is that it reinforces the notion that Aboriginal education either is or should be only about the instruction of Aboriginal students. Unfortunately, the rich potential for Aboriginal education to become an important process for meaning-making and cultural bridging, and to offer an invaluable lived experience for all students – Aboriginal and non-Aboriginal – is greatly diminished. Instead, the focus turns towards the education of "underachieving" Aboriginal students in which the main goal is to bring these individuals "up to par" with their non-Aboriginal peers, particularly in the high profile subject areas of mathematics, the sciences, and English or French literacy/language arts.

2. The class- and gender-based inequities, along with racist assumptions found in many standardized tests and testing procedures have been well documented in the research literature (Canadian Teachers' Federation, 2004: 13-14; Kohn, 2000: 36; Sacks, 1999: 113). Moreover, these kinds of evaluation tools and methods tend to examine aspects of learning that are readily quantifiable, thereby inadvertently diminishing the value of students' critical and creative thinking skills, social skills, and other learning "outcomes" that are much more difficult to measure (Canadian Teachers' Federation, 2004: 11; Jones, 2004: 585).

3. A nearly exclusive focus on academic performance outcomes and results in the predominant accountability models diverts attention from learning processes and, in the context of

Indigenous knowledge, the ethical dimension of knowing. This approach also often fails to take into consideration the highly individualized and differentiated opportunities to learn that are typically evident among a classroom of students and which affect achievement levels.

4. Accountability models sometimes inadvertently create what may be understood as a dilemma of negative reports. If members of historically oppressed or marginalized population groups in a society perform relatively poorly on an accountability measure, how should those results be reported? Should negative results be reported at all? On the one hand, a report may prompt action to address the inequities that underlie the results. On the other hand, these kinds of reports may further contribute to the stereotypes and stigmatization that are experienced by the group in question, especially when the reports are unaccompanied by any critical analysis of the biases, ideological assumptions, and political motives that are associated with the accountability model being used.

5. An "outcomes" based accountability environment that is characterized by standardized student achievement testing may have detrimental consequences – intended and unintended – for teachers' professional identity and practice. This culture of testing too often leads to a relentless criticism of teachers' professional judgment and competence. It can frustrate teachers' efforts to act in the best educational interests of individual students and contribute to the over-simplification (particularly in the news media) of education, students' needs, and teachers' roles. Given the complexities of Aboriginal education, in which teachers are trying to adapt their teaching practice in ways that respect and affirm multiple worldviews, values, and norms, this is especially problematic.

Aboriginal teachers may find themselves in a particularly awkward predicament, both professionally and personally.

They are often burdened with an expectation on the part of many administrators and teaching colleagues that they are the de facto experts regarding First Nations and Métis cultures and histories and that they should take a leadership role in all aspects of Aboriginal education (St. Denis et.al., 1998: 4-6; Bouvier, 2004: 39). To resist these inappropriate and often overwhelming expectations takes considerable courage. At the same time, however, Aboriginal teachers are given the message (sometimes none too subtly) that if they do not show leadership on Aboriginal education initiatives, no one else will. This dilemma is compounded by an accountability environment where what is "really important" are certain subjects (mathematics, the sciences, and language arts/ literacy), not Aboriginal education.

For many Aboriginal as well as non-Aboriginal teachers, perhaps the most distressing aspects of the testing culture may be the negative effects on their everyday classroom activities and especially on the relationships that they form with their students. As part of their work, most teachers realize how important it is to create a learning environment in which students feel safe – physically, psychologically and emotionally – and where trust is normative. Standardized testing can undermine this sense of safety and trust when students, particularly individuals who already feel marginalized in the education system, believe that the teacher's primary role is to evaluate or judge them. It is often difficult for young people to understand the differences between having their academic achievement evaluated and being judged as persons. The problem is compounded when, as is the case with many standardized formats, the testing criteria and processes are experienced by students (Aboriginal and non-Aboriginal) as being fairly arbitrary, externally imposed upon the classroom, a generally unpleasant ritual, and seemingly disconnected from their future learning activities.

A related dilemma is that in this kind of environment the teachers themselves begin to feel that they are not trusted, not only by some students, but also by parents, employers, and the general public. Can teachers feel safe about their jobs when there is so much pressure to improve students' test scores and, in some jurisdictions, to rank and rate schools accordingly? Is it safe for teachers to take risks in their work, and in the context of Aboriginal education to explore different worldviews, new forms of knowledge, and alternative perspectives? Can they continue to act on their ideals as teachers – the "heart of teaching" that motivated them to enter the profession and guides their work with the whole child – when the political focus is on academic results, results, results? Are they trusted to demonstrate professional accountability by assessing their students' learning in constructive ways that facilitate further growth (Jamison, 2002: 34-37)?

Or does the culture of testing demoralize everyone who is directly involved and foster cynicism within the education system? Does it produce technocratic teachers – Aboriginal as well as non-Aboriginal – who must conform to the values and logic of functional (means-ends) rationality (e.g., technical efficiency, effectiveness, quantifiable achievement, cost/benefit analysis, specialization of roles) at the expense of the kinds of non-functional values (e.g., meaningfulness, compassion, creativity, empathy, joy) that many teachers see as essential to their work and everyday relationships with students? To adapt Weber's (1958: 182) "iron cage" analogy, are teachers becoming "specialists without spirit, professionals without heart"?

CONCLUSION: THE PROMISE AND THE CHALLENGE

Taken together, these dilemmas and contradictions raise some important questions about the future of both Aboriginal education and accountability processes. For Aboriginal education, one cumulative effect of these difficulties that we have identified may be to diminish and distort its full potential. A key promise of Aboriginal education is that it can honour, respect, and in many ways protect the "wholeness" of Indigenous knowledge and Aboriginal cultures. At the level of the individual, this promise has particular significance for First Nations, Métis, and Inuit students, but as we have suggested, non-Aboriginal students would also benefit greatly from having a deep understanding of this knowledge.

At the societal level, the other major promise in Aboriginal education, broadly conceptualized, is that it can point the way out of the increasingly rigid socio-economic and psychological constraints – the "iron cage" of functional rationality and instrumentality – that characterize the dominant and global economic order, publicly as well as privately funded education systems (as demonstrated by the heightened focus on "education as job training," "raising the bar of student achievement levels" and so on) and even many aspects of personal relationships. When fully realized, Aboriginal education can offer insights into alternative values and norms, as well as different ways of experiencing physical, social, and political worlds and relating as human beings to "place" and other people.

We are not suggesting that Aboriginal worldviews and cultures are inherently superior, either cognitively or normatively, to those of other societies. Nor do we hold to a sentimental or utopian notion about the practical limitations of Aboriginal education (or any form of education, for that matter) in serving as a catalyst for social change. Rather, our point is that Aboriginal education is one important process through which individuals from very different backgrounds, especially young persons, can respectfully engage the pluralism of modern life, "'create' a space between the Indigenous and Western worlds, the separation betwixt cultures and worldviews" (Ermine, 2005: 1), and direct more attention to the inequities and complex human needs of a rapidly evolving global society.

If the promise of Aboriginal education is to be acted upon, a major challenge will be to overcome or at least minimize the dilemmas and contradictions that stem from the accountability movement. At the same time, there is a need to withstand the fairly powerful political pressures (some of which appear to have the support of some First Nations, Métis, and Inuit leaders in response to the often overwhelming inequities and pressing economic realities that Aboriginal peoples experience) that are associated with the accountability movement and which threaten, whether intentionally or not, to reduce Aboriginal education within Saskatchewan and other provinces into becoming little more than yet another "jobs training" instrument or an elective in a secondary school curriculum. In this environment, even the appropriateness of Aboriginal curricula may continue to undergo unusually intense scrutiny and screening from officials and educators who apply the narrowly defined standards of the "accountability-as-standardized-testing" model. As some critics have noted, "this aggressive gate-keeping of 'standards' has repeatedly challenged the legitimacy of Aboriginal knowledge and values, imposing an assimilative cultural agenda that is both pervasive and coercive" (Castellano, Davis, and Lahache, 2000: 251).

But perhaps there is an opportunity here that still needs to be explored. The dilemmas and contradictions that we have identified pose a challenge not only for Aboriginal education, but also for the future of accountability. Other critiques of the results-oriented testing model of accountability have highlighted its shortcomings and short sightedness. The fundamental incompatibility between this type of model and the philosophy of Aboriginal education, broadly defined, lends additional weight to the questioning of what has become the dominant accountability model. Put differently, educational accountability as it is currently practiced may be facing a crisis of legitimacy. The Indigenous knowledge, values, and norms that are inherent to Aboriginal education could inform the development of meaningful alternatives that are, it is hoped, much more perceptive about the human qualities of education and the pluralism of modern societies.

BIBLIOGRAPHY

Battiste, M. (1995). Introduction. In Battiste, M. & Barman, J. (Eds.). *First Nations Education in Canada: The Circle Unfolds*. Vancouver: UBC Press.

Battiste, M. (1998). "Enabling the Autumn Seed: Toward a Decolonized Approach to Aboriginal Knowledge, Language, and Education." *Canadian Journal of Native Education*, 22(1): 16-27.

Battiste, M., ed. (2000). *Reclaiming Indigenous Voice and Vision*. Vancouver: UBC Press.

Battiste, M. & Henderson, J. (2000). *Protecting Indigenous Knowledge and Heritage: A Global Challenge*. Saskatoon: Purich Publishing Ltd.

Battiste, M. & McLean, S. (2005). "State of First Nations Learning." Paper prepared for the Canadian Council on Learning. Saskatoon: Aboriginal Education Research Centre.

B.C. Teachers' Federation (2002). *Aboriginal Education – Beyond Words*. Vancouver.

Biesta, G. (2004). "Education, Accountability, and the Ethical Demand: Can the Democratic Potential of Accountability be Regained?" *Educational Theory*, 54(3): 233-250.

Bouvier, R. (2004). "The Critical Role of Aboriginal Educators." *Orbit*, 34(1): 38-40.

Canadian Council on Learning (2005). "State of Aboriginal Learning." Background paper for the National Dialogue on Aboriginal Learning, Ottawa, November 13-14, 2005.

Canadian Teachers' Federation (2004). *Educational Accountability with a Human Face*. Ottawa.

Carr-Stewart, S. (2003). "School^PLUS and Changing Demographics in Saskatchewan: Toward Diversity and Educational Communities." *Canadian Journal of Native Education*, 27(1): 223-234.

Castellano, M.B., Davis, L. & Lahache, L. (Eds.). *Aboriginal Education: Fulfilling the Promise*. Vancouver: UBC Press.

Council of Ministers of Education, Canada (2005). "Priority Action Plans: Aboriginal Education." Ottawa. URL: www.cmec.ca.

Erasmus, G. (2002). "2002 Lecture." Speech presented at the LaFontain-Baldwin Symposium, Vancouver, March 8, 2002. URL: http://www.operation-dialogue.com/lafontaine-baldwin/e/2002_speech_1.html

Ermine, W. (2005). "Ethical Space: Transforming Relations." (Discussion paper.) URL: www.traditions.gc.ca/docs_disc_ermine_e.cfm

Froese-Germain, B. (2005). "Teacher Perspectives on Educational Accountability." *Our Schools/Our Selves*, 14 (3): 57-76.

Hébert, Yvonne (2000). "The State of Aboriginal Literacy and Language Education." In Castellano, M.B., Davis, L. & Lahache, L. (Eds.). *Aboriginal Education: Fulfilling the Promise*, pp. 55-75. Vancouver: UBC Press.

Hodgson-Smith, K. (2005). "State of Métis Nation Learning." Paper prepared for the Canadian Council on Learning. Saskatoon: Infinity Research Inc.

Jamison, P. (2002). *Teacher Decision Making in Student Evaluation*. Regina: Saskatchewan School Trustees Association.

Jones, K. (2004). "A Balanced School Accountability Model: An Alternative to High-Stakes Testing." *Phi Delta Kappan*, 85(8): 584-590.

Kohn, A. (2000). *The Case Against Standardized Testing*. Portsmouth, NH: Heinemann.

Melnechenko, L. & Horsman, H. (1998). *Factors that Contribute to Aboriginal Students' Success in School in Grades Six to Nine*. Regina: Saskatchewan Education.

Meyer, M. (2005). "Remembering Our Future: Hawaiian Epistemology and the Specifics of Universality." *International Indigenous Journal*, 1(1): 49-55.

Richards, J. & Vining, A. (2004). "Aboriginal Off-Reserve Education: Time for Action." *C.D. Howe Institute Commentary*, 198 (April): 1-27.

Robertson, H. (2003). "Decolonizing Schools." *Phi Delta Kappan*, 84(7): 552-553.

Sacks, P. (1999). *Standardized Minds*. Cambridge, MA: Perseus Books.

Saskatchewan Learning (1989). *Indian and Métis Education Policy from Kindergarten to Grade XII*. Regina.

Saskatchewan Learning (2003). *Building Partnerships: First Nations and Métis Peoples and the Provincial Education System*. Regina.

Saskatchewan Learning (2004a). "The Learning Community in Aboriginal Education: 2004-2007 Priorities Report". *Report of the Aboriginal Education Provincial Advisory Committee*. Regina.

Saskatchewan Learning (2004b). *Saskatchewan Education Indicators: Kindergarten to Grade 12*. Regina.

Smith, M. (2001). "Relevant Curricula and School Knowledge: New Horizons." In Binda, K.P. (Ed.) with Calliou, S. *Aboriginal Education in Canada: A Study in Decolonization*, pp. 77-88. Mississauga: Canadian Educators' Press.

St. Denis, V. & Hampton, E. (2002). "Literature Review on Racism and the Effects on Aboriginal Education." Paper prepared for the Minister's National Working Group on Education, Indian and Northern Affairs Canada.

St. Denis, V., Bouvier, R., & Battiste, M. (1998). *Okiskinahamakewak: Aboriginal Teachers in Publicly Funded Schools*. Regina: Saskatchewan Education Research Networking Project.

Weber, M., translated by Talcott Parsons (1958). *The Protestant Ethic and the Spirit of Capitalism*. New York: Charles Scribner's Sons.

Weber, M., edited by Talcott Parsons (1964). *The Theory of Social and Economic Organization*. New York: Free Press.

Wotherspoon, T. (2004). "Competitiveness and Inclusion: Teachers' Work in a Knowledge-Based Economy." (Department of Sociology, University of Saskatchewan. Unpublished paper.)

NOTES

[1] It is important to keep in mind, however, that Aboriginal status is determined through the self-identification of students or their parents. Actual numbers of Aboriginal students in Saskatchewan will be higher than the official figures indicate since not all individuals choose to self-identify their status. It should also be noted that very few individuals in Saskatchewan self-identify as Inuit. For an analysis of the demographic changes taking place in Saskatchewan and the implications for Aboriginal education, see Carr-Stewart (2003).

[2] These facilities are administered, within the sphere of the federal government's jurisdiction, by First Nations or tribal councils and are not part of the publicly funded provincial pre-K-12 education system.

[3] Meyer (2005: 54), for example, notes the following central tenets of Hawaiian Indigenous epistemology:

1. Knowledge that endures is a spiritual act that animates and educates.
2. We are earth and our awareness of how to exist with it is an extension of this idea.
3. Our senses are culturally shaped, offering us distinct pathways to reality.
4. Knowing something is bound to how we develop a relationship with it.
5. Function is vital with regard to knowing something.
6. Intention shapes our language and creates our reality.
7. Knowing is embodied and in union with cognition.

[4] As the policy from which the four principles in this excerpt are taken was written in 1989, some of the language and phrasing used may be somewhat outdated. For many years, the Department of Learning has had a provincial advisory committee (currently known as the Aboriginal Education Provincial Advisory Committee) that is comprised of a broad range of representatives from the educational community, including First Nations and Métis educational organizations. Among its other functions, this committee works to ensure that policy is kept current and that, through its reports and recommendations to the provincial government, new policy and program needs are addressed. (See Saskatchewan Learning, 2004a.)

[5] See, for example, the overview of the new "Three 'Rs'" in the Department of Learning's publication, School^PLUS^ Progress (Saskatchewan Learning, 2005).

[6] Max Weber's (1964: 117) analysis of the formal (means-ends) rationality and instrumentality that underlies the structure and routine operations of most social institutions (including educational institutions) and that characterizes much of modern life, is instructive here. Karl Mannheim extended this work and concluded that a functional rational "mentality" involves the development of generalized standards, along with a focus on technical efficiency, effectiveness, performance criteria, cost/benefit analysis, and so on, not only in the marketplace, but in other institutions as well. (See Karl Mannheim, Man and Society in an Age of Reconstruction, 1940. New York: Harcourt Brace.) What may be called technical-managerial accountability models in education are generally based, though not necessarily consciously so, upon these kinds of functional rational values and norms.

[7] See, for example, Richards and Vining's (2004: 19-20) call for strengthened standards and province-wide tests in core subjects for all students and for "the prime minister and the premiers to rethink their Aboriginal policy priorities and raise the importance accorded to education outcomes" (p. 23).

[8] The Council of Ministers of Education, Canada (2005: 1), for example, has recently announced that a priority in the area of "Aboriginal education" is "to find new and varied ways of working together to improve the outcomes of Aboriginal students in both the elementary-secondary and postsecondary education systems"

Education Reform in Latin America's Southern Cone: Points of Resistance

A MULTI-UNION RESEARCH TEAM FROM ARGENTINA, BRAZIL, CHILE, AND URUGUAY

What follows is an excerpt from a document entitled Education and Reform in Southern Cone Countries. *The study examines recent education trends in Argentina, Brazil, Chile and Uruguay and reveals some of the dramatic consequences of the neo-liberal project imposed on almost all of Latin America in recent years. It was produced by a multi-union research team made up of representatives of the Confederation of Education Workers of Argentina, the National Confederation of Education Workers (Brazil), the Teachers College (Chile), and the National Federation of High School Teachers and the Association of Employees of the Universidad del Trabajo (Uruguay). The work was funded by several Canadian teachers' organizations – the British Columbia Teachers' Federation (BCTF), the Québec Union Central (CSQ) and the Ontario Secondary School Teachers' Federation (OSSTF). It was translated by Ruth Leckie and Carmen Miranda-Barrios. Coordination of the teams' work was carried out by the Latin American Observatory on Education Policies of the Laboratory of Public Policies (Rio de Janeiro – Buenos Aires) under the responsibility of Pablo Gentili and Daniel Suárez. Project Assistants were Florencia Stubrin, Julián Gindin and Paola Ferrari. The document's authors would like to thank Richard Langlois, Jocelyn Berthelot, Larry Kuehn and Steve Stewart, as well as their organizations, without whose solidarity and support this project would not have been possible.*

During this process of shared analysis, an essential aspect that emerged was the particular character of the conflict occurring within the different national education systems of the Southern Cone. Given each country's different history and the particular conditions under which each country experienced the implementation of neo-liberal reformist policies in education, the common feature that we identified was resistance. This resistance has had as its central focus the education reforms that were designed by international organizations, which pushed the neo-liberal (economic) and neo-conservative (political) agenda in our countries with few adaptations to national particularities.

The study carried out by our unions allowed us to identify a series of basic characteristics of education reform that reveal how clearly it has failed in our countries. This failure is now being covered up or justified in one way or another by our respective governments.

However, we are not only interested in describing the problem in order to understand more fully the realities of our region. We also want this collective process of constructing knowledge to lead to common strategies for mobilizing education workers to work towards real educational transformation in each country of the Southern Cone, as well as in other sectors and in our neighbouring countries. We need strategies that do not repeat the political errors of the past and that are the result of critical analysis of what has gone on in order to build alternatives that include all social sectors in the process of change.

From our analysis of the effects of neo-liberal education reform in Southern Cone countries, we have identified four key areas on which to focus in our final reflections and conclusions. These areas are: the role of the State; education funding; national education systems; and teachers' working conditions.

THE ROLE OF THE STATE

The national reports show how the process of education reform occurred in a context in which the function of the State was being redefined according to the basic principles of the neo-liberal ideology. The economic life of society was to be organized in new, capitalist terms, according to which it was necessary to return to the market the power that the welfare state had taken from it. Thus, a simultaneous process began in which, on the one hand, the State was reorganized internally, and, on the other, its role in the general management of social, economic and political life was radically changed. Within this process the dominant economic groups with transnational capital played a hegemonic role in the neo-liberal offensive.

Education reforms were carried out in the Southern Cone in the context of globalization – characterized by the expansion of global capitalism through the transnationalization of capital. The consequences of this process are the concentration and centralization of wealth as well as the consolidation of and increase in structural inequalities. This shift to a global economy could not have been carried out without changes to the role of nation states. As a labour movement we must expose and denounce the fact that this change in the role of the State is due as much to the active willingness of the governments of our respective countries to implement policies of structural adjustment as it is to the pressures of globalization to which those administrations found themselves subject. Local governments took it upon themselves to fulfill the requirements of the neo-liberal policies being pushed by international financial organizations without placing any limits on such changes.

Economic liberalization was expressed in a series of policies whose "scientific veracity" was seen as indisputable. International financial institutions and their intellectuals and think tanks carried out a "cultural war" which, at least at first, they seemed to be winning. They seemed to have found the standard prescription for overcoming stagnation and poverty. These policies included, among others, the indiscriminate opening up of national economies to both trade and the free circulation of international capital. More specifically, they have meant the concentration of huge profits in the dominant countries or in those places where they are assured of maintaining and expanding their power. The weakening of the state and its national production apparatus was carried out through the privatization of public corporations and the deregulation of services. Thus, market structures were brought into the state, which became little more than a big game reserve for the most powerful economic groups. As exploitation of workers increased and their organizing strength diminished, policies to relax and deregulate the labour force were brought in and state institutions that had guaranteed the protection of certain labour rights were either reduced or dissolved. It is within this context of a neo-liberal offensive that the reorganization of "social spending," including education, took place. And it is within this context of a neo-liberal offensive that we must try to apprehend, understand and explain the education reforms now underway.

We conclude that the result was not simply a reduction in the size and strength of governments, as is usually claimed by neo-liberal proponents. Rather, what we have seen is a real change in terms of how the state intervenes in public policy. To a greater and lesser degree, depending on the country, governments began to abandon their responsibility of redistributing the wealth of their countries, as well as their role in the protection of the social rights of the poorer sectors of society. The dominant classes in the different countries of the region picked up on the neo-liberal discourse against workers and held up the corporate model of organization as the ideal to be imitated.

The neo-liberal state came into being as a result of the reorganization of the state by governments who embraced this ideology and which were the local expression of powerful economic groups linked to transnational capital. Through this process, they also transformed civil society, particularly in its relation to the state. At no point did the state cease to play an active role. What did change, however, was the way it participated in managing the economic and political accumulation of power by certain economic groups. In terms of the relationship of these groups, and of business in general, with workers, the neo-liberal state became the overseer of the most brutal exploitation and social exclusion. The trend was for the state to act more as a manager working in the economic interest of transnational corporations than as a regulator placing limits on voracious capital.

In the area of education, the process began with an attempt to negate the idea of education as a social right. Educational activity was conceived as a service in which knowledge acquired the character of a commodity. Governments worked actively to weaken the belief in public education as a national public project that aspires to form citizens who take an active role in the defense of their rights, their dignity and their future. They looked for any possible way to transform education into an activity guided by the rules of the marketplace, leaving the possibility of going to school up to the particular social circumstances of the individual.

It is important to note that this obviously anti-popular ideological transformation required a radical change in a mentality that had for years believed in the importance of defending the rights of the most vulnerable. Neo-liberal governments prioritized this aspect of their ideological offensive in their actions and corresponding provision of resources.

Our research has shown that with this new role for the state in the neo-liberal context, education policies have been characterized by the coexistence of two apparently contradictory processes. The first, and most developed, is the financial and administrative decentralization of education systems. The other is the process of centralizing pedagogical aspects of education in the national government, through evaluation, setting of curriculum and other measures that affect what goes on in the classroom. This centralization is perhaps the most common education policy in the region.

The neo-liberal state of the 1990s needed to carry out an ideological battle in order to justify the brutally regressive concentration of wealth and to reduce and reorganize social spending, which of course included education. As was noted above, they worked to weaken public support for public education and to reduce it to a simply compensatory role. To do this, they began the transfer of education to the private realm. The transfer of private funds to private educational institutions increased in all four countries of the region, as did private spending by teachers, parents and communities to maintain "free" public schools. All of this is consistent with seeing education as part of the economy and, thus, private. Each individual is responsible for his or her own failure or success. This ideology implies that if someone doesn't go to school, they can't claim that their general conditions stopped them from doing so. This would only be true in exceptional cases requiring targeted compensatory policies to address particularly unjust situations, which the state should assist in alleviating. This aspect of the neo-liberal offensive interacted (and continues to do so) with the different realities of the countries of the region and achieved various levels of success, depending on the particular forces at play in each country.

Seen in these terms, education can clearly be seen to be justifying and reinforcing existing inequalities and even making them worse. Within the context of this political and ideological project to organize education as if it were a private business, various concepts need to become hegemonic in order to justify the process. This battle continues, although not with the same virulence as at the beginning. Some aspects of the model have been modified, incorporating social needs and broadening the compensatory idea. The key ideas that now organize the mercantile discourse on education revolve around the concepts of equity, quality, efficiency, utility of knowledge, versatility, competencies, and a few others.

The concept of equity is an attempt to counter and even replace the idea of equality. In this way, the social and political nature of social inequalities is reduced to a question of a more equitable distribution of government subsidies. In the case of universities, free access is seen as not equitable because those who could pay are receiving a "state subsidy" just like those who cannot. This attitude is justified by saying that higher education has no broader social purpose and, in fact, students are capitalizing on their investment and generating a profit. If they are making a profit, then free education is a subsidy and therefore not equitable because those who could pay are not doing so. The solution would be a series of scholarships for those who are good candidates but are not able to study because of their financial situations. This example shows how neo-liberalism promotes the introduction of financial criteria in education through the concept of equity.

The concept of quality has had the greatest impact on the changing attitude towards educational issues and has lead to the evaluation of educational institutions, along with increased national control over curriculum. In terms of the pedagogical process, this concept of quality places all attention on the final product. Rather than discussing what goes on in the classroom as a space for the production of culture and citizenship, results are evaluated in terms of minimum knowledge acquired. This conceptual schema is consistent with an economic vision of education. The same can be said of most of the neo-liberal concepts of education mentioned above. The basic idea is that education is a business venture, and thus private, except when social compensation must be made to address inequities.

These conceptual tools, developed within different academic and ideological structures and then redefined by the neo-liberal technocrats of education reform, are also presented as the language of common sense, which is something, which we must also decipher and expose. We have observed how in our countries the process of education reform was accompanied by the co-opting of intellectuals by reformist authorities, by corruption in the distribution of jobs in the new structures created to carry out the reforms, and by the proliferation of NGOs, some of which have turned out to be the tangible expression of privatization and of the gradual abandonment by the state of essential areas of responsibility. As we have noted earlier, the process of globalization has placed education in the role of serving the needs of different markets, such as the educational, labour, and technological markets as well as those of international experts, publishers and others.

In the area of setting and developing curriculum, neo-liberal governments have assumed an active role. Educational analysis and proposals formulated in terms of education competencies are informing policy on curriculum and thus affecting the teaching process. They follow the new production model characterized by competition, versatility, an increasingly horizontal organization of work, flexibility, competitive teams and liberalization. These competencies organize teaching work in terms of its usefulness for the real world, remembering that in neo-liberal ideology the real world is defined by the market. Schools must prepare students to be able to function effectively under these terms. This means they must, to use the neo-liberal jargon, "acquire the adequate competencies." Changes to secondary education were conceptualized in this way to allow powerful economic interests to dictate educational processes such that the formation of human resources became the primary function of education. This new role for education, as reformulated in neo-liberal terms, not only abandons those objectives won by popular struggles (such as the conception of education as a human right and not simply a service), but also those connected to nationalism that had emerged from the ideological apparatus of the modern state. Education is now clearly related to finding a job within the prevailing economic model.

More than a decade of the implementation of education reforms in our countries (more than 20 in Chile), has set the stage for the failure of these policies. This failure is the result of one basic fact: our societies have seen an increase in the concentration of wealth, in unemployment, in poverty and in marginalization. The market has proven impotent in redistributing not only wealth but also cultural goods. Compensatory policies have managed to increase, in the majority of cases, the rate of enrolment but not to reduce the gap between those students and those others who gain access to the knowledge that plays a strategic role in maintaining social and political domination. Cultural elitism has been strengthened and with it, the instruments of social domination. Once again we see that capitalism, more specifically the market, does not lead to democratization.

At the beginning of the 1990s, structural reforms brought the ideas of the Washington Consensus into the field of education in an aggressive burst of modernity that, in spite of our objections, claimed it would "overcome underdevelopment and bring the countries of the region into the process of globalization" (according to a World Bank document). The reality, after more than a decade of structural adjustment, relaxation of labour laws and fragmentation of education systems is quite simply catastrophic and the resulting poverty is hitting the great majority of the population of the region.

In Latin America, the neo-liberal model is in deep crisis as a result of the strength of popular struggles against it. The growth of such resistance occurred as people began to see and experience what different popular movement sectors had been warning against all along. Policies to deregulate the market, to privatize public corporations and to relax labour standards only resulted in unemployment, extreme poverty and increased marginalization, just as had been predicted. Through these social struggles to defend the rights that were being violated, the neo-liberal model began to lose its legitimacy. As social conditions have worsened and resistance increased, the failure of the project has become visible. In this context of growing social exclusion, in which education was no exception, awareness is growing of the failure of neo-liberal reforms across the continent and in the Southern Cone in particular.

The strong activism of the popular movement opened up the possibility of alternative models of change for the countries of the Southern Cone and the rest of Latin America (Lula in Brazil, the electoral triumph of the Frente Amplio or Broad Front in Uruguay, Kirchner in Argentina). These are not "magic" solutions to the social problems weighing upon us, but they do open up a space for and legitimize a critical discussion of neo-liberalism. This makes it possible to develop alternative political strategies with a commitment to social justice, democracy and national dignity. However, the fact that neo-liberal reforms have failed does not mean they have gone away. It is still possible for governments to modify the model, giving it a more progressive aspect, but then continue to apply neo-liberal policies. This requires a double effort on the part of our union movement. On the one hand, we must continue to oppose and actively resist the type of education reform policies implemented in our countries. And at the same time, we must address ourselves, with pedagogical imagination, cultural creativity and popular democratic commitment, to the task of recreating critical political thought and action on educational alternatives to the neo-liberal model.

To do this we must remember that this resistance is not limited to the struggle of unions, but involves the opposition of society against the neo-liberal model – an opposition that has emerged from the real experience of seeing and feeling the growing impoverishment and marginalization in our daily lives and at the same time the increasing concentration of wealth in the hands of powerful economic groups and the cultural and political elites associated with them. The failure of education reform must be seen in a context of resistance and of a growing awareness that the benefits of education and knowledge are now meant only for the few, not for the majority, and that this in turn becomes an essential aspect of the power of the dominant minority.

In the face of this criticism, one line of defense for neo-liberalism has been to blame the teachers. But it has not been the "teacher factor" that has been an obstacle to reform, as some intellectuals have claimed. Rather, it is the fact that whenever there is inequality, policies to shift state powers to the marketplace only aggravate those inequalities. It is this deepening inequality that teachers and other sectors of the education community have rigorously opposed. If there had been no such resistance, things would undoubtedly be even worse.

Another line of defense for neo-liberalism in the face of this growing awareness of increasing inequality in education has been to point to the increase in the school enrolment rate, particularly at the secondary level. They say "Today there are more kids in school than ever." While this may well be true, it must be added that, as our multi-union study has shown, the social and working conditions in schools have deteriorated, indicating an increasing differentiation in educational experiences according to the differing socio-economic situations of the participants. The number of teachers in relative terms is lower, there are not more and better spaces and times for learning and teaching work is carried out under increasingly impoverished conditions. Enrolment may be up, but this is not due to a good model, but rather to different social processes that are underway as the population continues to believe in the importance of sending children to school and the labour movement continues to defend public education as one of the last bastions from which to defend the idea of public spaces. What we are questioning are the attitudes of individualism, pragmatism and of social selection and stratification that neo-liberalism has brought to education and which we need to reverse.

In conclusion, this summary of changes to the role of the state through neo-liberal policies has shown two things clearly. The first is that it is not true that the state has been reduced in order to give way to the market. In reality, what has happened is that its role has been modified in order to produce and reproduce the conditions that guarantee the functioning of the market in favour of the dominant transnational economic groups. The second is that neo-liberal education reform policies have resulted in greater inequality and, as a consequence, have provoked a growing resistance that is impeding their implementation and undermining their legitimacy and that of all neo-liberal policies.

EDUCATION FUNDING

Given the analysis and conclusions of our research, we want to make clear that the problem of funding cannot and should not be reduced simply to a question of numbers. Through their funding policies, which we see as one of the key instruments for the implementation of education reforms, the neo-liberal reformers also tried to redefine the role of the state. These policies are constructed upon the huge external debts of our countries and are part of a context in which such policies are imposed on the world's economies in a differentiated way, with particularly serious effects on most developing countries.

Education funding did not decrease in Latin America, in fact in many countries spending increased, but the fundamental problem has been in its composition and distribution. As our research has shown, throughout this process there has been a re-directing of spending that has not guaranteed either the democratization or the improvement of educational conditions for either the general population or for education workers in particular.

An important aspect of financing is public spending. It is important to clarify that the main problem is not simply one of how much is spent, but rather of how it is distributed. What has really happened during the period of education reform is that the increase in public spending did not keep up with the increase in enrolment nor the expansion of the overall education system nor the new complexities of the increase in number and age of students. The allocation of resources and policies of budget distribution and allocation also contributed to the deterioration of the working conditions of teachers, to a widening of the gap between different social sectors and to the impoverishment of the public schools at the heart of an increasingly fragmented and disorganized education system.

In terms of the quantitative aspects of public spending, we should also point out that only looking at an overall increase in spending can hide the differing situations experienced in different jurisdictions. Such is the case in Argentina where the increase in spending in Buenos Aires raises the total amount of education spending but also obscures the huge disparity between that jurisdiction and the other provinces in the country. It is also important, when attempting to understand the significance of the increases to public spending in the 1990s, to remember how extreme the deterioration of the 1980s had been.

In terms of the qualitative aspects of public spending, we have seen a clear shift in spending priorities away from expenditures on personnel and towards subsidies to private institutions.

The decentralization of education funding is another aspect that is important to discuss in our political conclusions. We have seen how it took different forms in each country and was implemented through transference laws and other measures of shifting responsibility to provinces and municipalities. The transfer of institutions and personnel from national jurisdictions to the provinces/municipalities was not accompanied by budget allocations that were sufficient to cover the real costs of these services, especially if we consider the deterioration that had occurred during the 1980s in terms of physical infrastructures and salaries as well as the increase in demand for education. These transfers certainly made the financial problems of the provinces much worse.

The discourse used to justify this transfer of services claimed that national governments would guarantee that the transferred services would be delivered with full numerical coverage, high pedagogical quality and equity throughout the different jurisdictions. However, the real incentive for the transfer of education services from national governments was fiscal and political. In terms of the former, there was a visible effect on public spending in the provinces – their budgets grew as a result of the inclusion of education. In terms of the latter, it was an attempt to dilute the political responsibility of national governments and shift it to provinces and municipalities. Neo-liberal governments hoped to reap two benefits from this. First, to protect themselves from the loss of legitimacy that would result from their inability to respond to the educational needs of the community. Secondly, they maintained other ways of controlling pedagogical issues in cultural areas and as they related to the needs of capital.

Privatization, deregulation, contracting out and a general opening up of the economy were the strategies used by neo-liberal political programmes in our countries to shift from public entities to the economic elite the power to regulate and intervene in various aspects of society. One of these aspects, which has been the focus of our research, is education. The increase in transfers of public funds to private institutions and their overall expansion into our education systems has been a result of the implementation of neo-liberal reforms. Neo-liberal discourse promotes the principle of a family's freedom to select the school of their choice. This is one of the guiding principles of the Chicago School and goes along with their theories of human capital and the commodification of knowledge. In fact, the principle of free choice is in direct conflict with the impossibility of choice in a population where the majority live in poverty. In this type of situation, people must maintain their solidarity in the face of unemployment and the challenges of daily survival. Cooperation and solidarity are much more valuable tools in the context of marginalization and poverty than the individualistic concept of free choice.

This favourable climate for expanding private spaces is possible because of a vision of the state that externalizes its own functions. This economic model includes the contracting out of services, which is one way to introduce the market and the ideology of powerful economic forces into state projects. This trend can be seen in the proliferation of new private spaces (cafeterias, consultants, NGOs, institutes, etc.) that are influencing and even directly intervening in decisions on education policy. Many of these are the same institutions that produce the consumption-based cultural and ideological concepts that circulate in the parallel market of the techno-bureaucracy of the education ministries in our countries and in the multinational organizations that finance national governments. This development was promoted through the conditions of these same international finance institutions. They not only made it possible for private institutions to enter into the field of education, but their recommendations became the means by which education policies were implemented.

In all these aspects of funding policies we can see that the objective has been to change the political and ideological direction of the state's involvement in the education systems of the region. Promises of equality and accessibility were abandoned and in the process, existing educational inequalities were made worse. Protest and resistance has made the inadequacy of funding visible and today, in the face of these social demands and of the proof that the reforms have failed, funding is now increasingly being channeled to address the most urgent cases of inequality. This targeted approach attempts to compensate for the undesired and unjust effects of neo-liberal policies. International financial institutions are promoting this approach and are even providing credit to fund such programmes. The general direction of education policies in the region, however, continues to be neo-liberal, albeit a somewhat modified version.

EDUCATION SYSTEMS

With an understanding of the State's new role as analyzed in the first part of these conclusions, we can see that the State's position on funding policies is in direct contradiction to its relationship with the education system, especially in terms of pedagogy. In other words, in contrast to its decentralized function at the administrative and financial level, it takes a highly centralized role in political-pedagogical decisions, particularly those regarding curriculum policy and the evaluation of those involved in the education system.

The whole design and implementation of the reform process was centralized and directed by the official, centralized bureaucracy, without taking into account any suggestions from teachers or the educational community, disallowing any real consultation and direct participation. The participatory spaces that were available were apparently democratic, but, in fact, they were intended to legitimize the reforms or to introduce modifications as already defined by specialists and officials following the "recommendations" of international financial organizations. As noted above, two mechanisms used to carry out pedagogical centralization were curriculum and the evaluation.

Ideological hegemony is a key aspect of the neo-liberal education system. With this concept of education in mind, the curriculum was organized around a centralized notion of those contents considered to be basic. This process of changing curriculum contents happened all over the region, and was based on the scientific, technological, and cultural transformations that had taken place since the postwar period and that are now being expressing through globalization. Technocratic criteria predominated in the elaboration of these contents and public discussion around them was limited. Teachers were not invited to participate in the process.

Once these contents had been established, the new directives and materials were delivered to teaching staff through curricular guidelines, textbooks and training. Many education technocrats were used in the preparation of this material, and often private or public institutions or "experts" were contracted out to produce the curricular guidelines. At this stage of the process, as well, teachers, parents, students and popular institutions from the region were again excluded from participating in the curriculum design. Through the training sessions, the contents were further developed for classroom implementation. The commercial aspect of the process increased at this stage, and there was no space for discussion of its effects, since the whole process was now situated at the private and market level. Because of new requirements, teachers now needed the credits they obtained by attending the training sessions, and government-contracting mechanisms were allied with the training market. Finally, textbooks were the instruments by which lesson plans, designed with absolutely no input from teachers, were implemented. Salary and working conditions pushed teachers to use the textbooks even more, which ended up informing the ideological direction of classroom teaching.

The vision of knowledge as a product and as a form of individual capitalization is at the root of the curricular hegemony described above. This promotes an instrumental and pragmatic vision of knowledge that can only be expressed as a tool with which to perform in an already determined reality – that of the market. From this perspective, education is purely instrumental, preparing students to adapt to an order, which it is only possible to improve through minor technical changes, but which in its essence is definite and unchangeable. This is the philosophy of the "end of history." The implicit pedagogy in neo-liberal education policy aims at converting the student into a passive subject who has to learn knowledge that was produced in another place and is valid only as long as it is useful. This neo-liberal ideal falls flat in the face of reality, in particular with the reality of young people. Students do not adapt in a passive way, much less do they passively accept what it is being taught. Schools are having more internal conflicts and debate regarding education as the crisis increases. To the complexity of this crisis is added the growing development of a two-tiered school system, depending on the participants' social and economic conditions.

In recent years, we have seen a major internal conflict within education systems. Neo-liberalism claims to have resolved this crisis in an administrative way, with schools being run as businesses and school principals being pushed to act as managers. Another way has been to blame teachers, focusing on their supposed lack of knowledge and on their inability to understand the new situation of youth in an era of globalization and a "society of knowledge." On this last point, neo-liberal discourse can easily be confused with others of a more "progressive" character. In this way, a capitalist social, political and cultural education system has no responsibility towards any particular country or for all the contradictions that this generates. However, the most important thing is that debate is growing, and it is more and more possible to clearly point out the weaknesses of neo-liberal solutions to school conflicts. Also in this context, we can talk about an important cultural resistance in which teachers can play an increasingly important role.

Another mechanism for ensuring the ideological hegemony of the didactic processes that teachers carry out in their workplaces is national evaluation. These centrally designed and administrated standardized exams are also meant to contribute to the creation of an "education market" where the driving element would be competition for quality. The neo-liberal ideal, in this context, is to have a school "ranking system" developed through parents' preferences and inter-school competition organized through evaluations. This ranking idea, created out of the evaluation process, is designed to develop the principle of free choice of schools that we mentioned above. This, in turn, will require a system of subsidizing demand that will replace support for the public education system. We will look at these two objectives of evaluation.

It is clear that the use of evaluation for ideological control has had and continues to have a significant impact on teachers' work in the classroom. In practice, this mechanism for ideological hegemony centres on the "final product" of the didactic process, with learning seen as quantifiable, measurable and comparable. The teaching process itself is not considered or is seen simply as a "black box" and thus there is no democratic (or other) discussion of different teaching methods and the ideological role that teaching materials have. Because all of these are to be provided by the market, there can be no public discussion of them. This is probably the place where teachers' work is most impacted by the system because they feel so pressured by the so-called "final results". Another objective of these evaluation processes is to affect the definition of schools' curriculum, working as a control mechanism and pushing underground any discussion of institutional autonomy. The result is that teachers end up teaching what is going to be evaluated, which is a decision of the national government.

It is not at all clear how important national evaluations are for parents in their decision-making. They are probably useful for those with the economic possibility of selecting the school of their choice. The popular sectors, for whom poverty is a big issue, do not have any alternative other than sending their children only to the schools they can afford. For these sectors the school "market" is an impossibility. However, we cannot generalize about this situation in all countries of the region, and we must also not ignore the different types of cultural resistance that teachers and educational communities are building to lessen the impact and, through struggle, guarantee the quality of the only school they can send their children to.

In the context of the profound changes that school systems have suffered in recent years, the issue of evaluation has taken on a new importance in pedagogical discourse. Nobody questions the need for evaluation, but when that evaluation is part of a technocratic discourse that in reality is linked to structural adjustment, a series of reductions is produced: evaluation becomes measurement and quality becomes efficiency. There is also a cultural battle going on here over the meaning of evaluation. An important task ahead is to reclaim the pedagogical tradition and to see evaluation as a process that allows us to understand a reality in order to change it.

We can see that there is a commonality in the different political actions carried out by the state, ideologically led by the dominant social classes and aimed at leading education in the direction defined by neo-liberal pedagogy. We can see the strength of neo-liberal hegemony in the way that teachers organize and carry out their work. We will analyze this in the next section.

TEACHERS' WORKING CONDITIONS

A quick historical overview of the social composition of the teaching sector and the building of its identity as workers shows that in the first half of the twentieth century, the economic value of teachers' work was limited to the state's implicitly appointed mission: the functions of literacy and citizenship. This was accepted by most until the beginning of the second half of the same century. During that period there were various milestones in the development of education workers' unions and labor organizations. Within the context of the idea of the state's mission, a growing and critical discourse of teachers as workers emerged.

The political and social transformations that emerged from the crisis of capitalism in the 1970s deeply affected our region. The subsequent reforms to the state mentioned above – in many cases introduced during dictatorships – and the economic crises that resulted from the savage hegemony of financial capital drastically lowered the standard of living of the middle class, forcing many teachers into poverty. It is important to mention here the high percentage of women involved and the fact that their salaries are often the most important in the family. In Argentina for example, a high percentage of women teachers are the main breadwinners in their houses. These changes in working conditions sped up a transformation of consciousness of class and opened up the possibility of thinking critically about ideological orientations, political hegemony and popular alternatives for teaching work. We think it important not to lose a dialectic perspective in this analysis.

The working class – formerly salaried, strong and united by the national projects of developed countries – started to fall apart and lost a large number of members because of changes due to globalization, privatization and labor flexibility that later were installed into the state structures of the region. Education workers, who had only recently joined the working class and organized into unions, began the conscious struggle to defend their salaries and to fight against the encroachment of commercial projects into their work. They also faced the challenges of the internal contradictions of class and citizenship at the heart of a model of government that has abandoned its historic role and simply sets the social, cultural and political stage for the developing hegemony of the neo-liberal project.

In our countries, as well as in the developed ones, labor market structures were re-configured as policies for education systems changed through the introduction of management criteria and labor flexibility into the running of schools. Governments launched an intense campaign to get rid of labor norms that had been historically won by the teachers, and that contained important regulations for teaching work, providing professional standards and stability. However, the resistance of teachers has been heroic. The progress of neo-liberalism varies within regions and even within different countries. In Chile, where teachers initially lost a lot of ground, their struggle has allowed them to make a significant recovery. In the full research project, of which this is a summary, it is possible to see the different achievements and failures of neo-liberalism.

It is important to understand that this new labor market is one of the mechanisms with which to impose a pedagogical hegemony. The commodification of knowledge that we mentioned above is key to this, as is the concept of study or training as an individual's capital investment. The neo-liberal project aims at designing an education market that appears to have as its goal the improvement of education quality. This appearance hides the ideological nature of the individualistic and competitive models imposed and that affect both teachers and students.

These ideological aspects of the problem can be seen in training programmes delivered by private companies and which act as a tool for meritocracy. The imposition of this kind of criteria with which to stratify teachers coheres with the new role of the knowledge market and the schools within it as they act to justify the economic groups that want to maintain their hegemony. Simply put, they claim that anybody can ascend socially and even attain power through knowledge. This neo-liberal ideal is very far from being a reality and is increasingly unlikely to ever becoming one.

This is why education workers' salaries were left with no parameters with which to determine their economic value (they were never clear) and were left vulnerable to the ups and downs of the cost of living and national currency devaluations. Teachers' salaries were never compared with workers' salaries in general because their work function was understood to be different. This differentiation, which was backed by governments, was accepted by many teachers, who were often middle class women. There are many instances of government officials who, responding to union demands for a salary increase, said that teachers did "intangible" work that "can not be measured in money."

Because teachers' official working day was shorter than that of other workers, the exhaustion and burn out produced by their work was not easily seen, and was not even recognized by most teachers themselves. Now the burden is intolerable. Students and teachers, as citizens, have been abandoned by the state. The ideological and cultural work done by the unions of the region has been important in building a class conscience. Our study showed that the true amount of time and social responsibility involved in teaching work has never been paid and constitutes an historic subsidizing of the state by education workers. This historic lack of economic recognition of teachers' work and responsibility is not unconnected to the unwillingness to accept a leading role for teachers in the design and direction of the didactic process.

The neo-liberal offensive's refusal to acknowledge teachers' actual pedagogical tasks adds to the impact on other socio-cultural and material aspects of the learning-teaching process. This can be seen in education budgets where the cost per student is the determining factor. The teacher appears as simply a material ingredient in the learning process and not as a pedagogical subject who teaches and learns within a didactic process and in the education system as a whole. This conception is far removed from the reality in the schools, which do not follow the logic of the system.

Schools have a functioning logic quite different from that of the larger system. It has been shown in many critical theory studies that the school is not a micro of the macro (system), neither as a concept nor as unit of explicative analysis of the whole. Thus, there is no economic value (real cost per school) placed on the daily and/or monthly "extra" contribution by teachers, cooks, janitors, administrative staff, families and the community. Through the voluntary contribution of time, money and/or other materials, "free public schools" are maintained. This is not just an economic problem; it is also important to expose the ideological elements that are at work in the teaching process.

This ignorance of the reality of our schools is also seen in the functions and tasks that education ministries have granted to the private sector, transforming education into profitable businesses including, among other services, construction, repair, publishing, graphic design, current technology, teacher training, and lesson plan "packages." Along with this, an entrepreneurial ideology towards the role of administrators is being promoted at all levels. Rather than attempting to understand the specificities of different education problems, there is a move to standardize needs into statistical units and then offer them to commercial bidders.

As long as there is no recognition of teachers' work in designing, carrying out and evaluating the learning process, the real time that all of these involve, or the material, social, cultural and ideological obstacles related to them, their psychological suffering will be ignored as well. These costs (economic, ideological and social) are not recognized at the current time so the deterioration of teaching work has only been measured in the loss of acquisitive capacity of teachers, ignoring the ever-increasing difficulty of carrying out their actual job. These aspects of the problem are seen as "moral" questions (negligence as a cause of absenteeism, lack of information-training as a cause of school failures, students' lack of respect, etc.) and not as labour conditions.

The Globalization of Education Policy and Practice in South Africa

SALIM VALLY AND CAROL ANNE SPREEN

Four years after the first democratic elections in South Africa, the Deputy Minister of Education (after quoting extensively from World Bank documents), implored South African educationists to "...go outside the classroom and engage ... about macroeconomic policies and strategies so that our curricula should, like good African soldiers, march in quick step with national economic imperatives" (Mkhatshwa 1999). The incongruity of Father Mkhatshwa's martial metaphor was matched by the South African state's embrace of neo-liberalism. The latter has severed continuity with the social justice ideals of South Africa's vibrant anti-apartheid education social movements and has not dramatically reduced inequality in the country's education system (for details of the "People's Education" movement under apartheid see Motala and Vally 2002).

Education policies over the last decade in South Africa have embraced three major perspectives: a demand for social justice, the need to be internationally competitive (with emphasis on science and technology to develop requisite "productive" skills) and the imperative of fiscal restraint (expressed as cost-containment measures and the increasing marketisation of education). The first perspective is dramatically at odds with the latter two, both of which are inspired by Human Capital Theory and South Africa's homegrown structural adjustment policy entitled Growth, Employment and Redistribution (GEAR). These two latter perspectives have resulted in an individualized educational culture where only the "fittest" survive, where knowledge is commodified for the market, and where subjects without a market niche are being phased out. They have also lead to major inequalities in South Africa's schools, reflecting the dramatic increase in inequality across the society as a whole since the adoption of the GEAR macroeconomic strategy.[1]

Encouragingly, in response to the impact of these policies, new and independent social movements have formed. They have established continuity with past movements and have exposed the hollowness of electoral promises around social delivery and corruption. They have also taken the lead in resisting neo-liberalism in all spheres of life.

The lack of service delivery around education, housing, health (particularly the HIV/AIDS pandemic), electricity, sanitation and water has once again made townships and informal settlements into "hotbeds of activism"; the Minister of Safety and Security recorded 5,800 citizen's protests in 2005 (Bond 2006). Out of these sustained protests, mass organizations such as the Landless People's Movement, the Anti-Privatisation Forum, Anti-Eviction Campaign, the Treatment Action Campaign and the Abahlali Base Mjondolo (Shack-dwellers movement) have arisen. These new social movements have increasingly allied themselves with local education resistance. The praxis of South Africa's Education Rights Project, discussed later in this chapter, is based on the struggles of these community organizations as well as on teacher unions, student organizations and poor parent bodies.

In examining the impact of the government's neo-liberalism in education and the rise of popular resistance to it, we want to focus on a number of specific policies: the National Qualification Framework, Curriculum 2005, the Further Education and Training (FET) policy, the Skills Development Strategy and the "downsizing" of teachers. We then want to explore responses to globalization by social movements and their efforts at restoring social justice in education. First, though, we want to try to understand what globalisation means. Is it, as some have argued, all "globaloney" – merely colonialism writ large – or are we in an epoch where the nation-state and national economies are fast becoming irrelevant and meaningless?

GLOBALISATION AND THE SOUTH AFRICAN STATE

While there is no doubt that the conditions imposed by the IMF/World Bank impact on the sovereignty of many developing nation states, international neo-liberal ideology itself takes place through the agency of the state. Recent developments in Venezuela, Uruguay and Bolivia show that all nation states are not naturally captives of globalisation and powerless to buck the trend. This does not mean that the imperatives of international competitiveness have not lessened the autonomous agency of individual states. What it does suggest, however, is that the limits on state policy are, to a significant extent, self-imposed. In many respects, governments are not obliged to become "midwives of globalisation" (Blackmore 1999). They often have a lot of room, as Dale (1999) puts it, to make "conscious" decisions about their economic futures. This is undoubtedly true for the current South African state. It could have and should have chosen another route toward development.

In South African education, as we shall see, the hopes for equitable schooling have been largely subverted by the imperatives of budgetary constraints linked to macroeconomic policies. The government had an option to fund the schools on the basis of rights instead of what has been officially presented as "available" resources and "rational" accounting techniques. (See Spreen and Vally 2006).

The neo-liberal option that was chosen emerged out of what Christie (1997) understands as a complex interplay between "global" and "local" political, socio-economic and cultural forces. The "negotiated compromise" left intact the power of the old economic elite, albeit through new configurations of power sharing at the level of the central state and on the ground of everyday political practice. In the end, much of post-apartheid educational policy has been narrowed to individualistic investment in human capital at the expense of democratic process. (Chisholm and Fuller 1996) Here are a few examples from these years.

GEAR AND THE RESURGENCE OF HUMAN CAPITAL THEORY:

Under the recent global resurgence of neo-liberal macro-economic perspectives, education is viewed as an economic investment in which students and workers are both a value added product and a means by which the economy is to be improved. Education and training is transformed into a panacea for economic performance as it is assumed that investment in human capital and technology will automatically increase productivity and skills on the shop floor. Also it conveniently transfers the responsibility for unemployment to individual deficiencies, implying that lack of employment is a reflection of a person's skills level and abilities instead of an intrinsic weakness of the economic structure and how employment is distributed.

Human capital theory (which was popular in the 1960's, and fell into disfavour after being heavily criticised by Marxists and dependency theorists in the 1970s and 1980s) has experienced a revival internationally in the present context of the rise of globalisation. But it remains an ideological hoax, which ends up blaming the victims. Knowledge becomes a commodity, which individuals may exchange for qualifications or credentials, which may be of value within a competitive market.

For Marginson "… Education cannot in itself generate capital movements or create wealth, except to the extent that it becomes a fully-fledged market commodity in its own right. The inevitable economic 'failure' of education, associated with credentialism and the demands of educators for more resources to fulfill their multiplying tasks, sustains the recurring policy cycle of illusion/disillusion, and its partner cycle of spending/cuts, that has dominated educational politics since the 1950s." She adds, that the difference between the cycle in the high modernization period and in the global era is that "while governmental illusions about education are as large as they ever were, government capacity to pay is not" (Marginson 1999).

This discourse of relating education to economic rationales and success in international competition permeates all the major post '94 educational reforms. Like other countries, GEAR promotes the marketisation of education, public-private partnerships, fiscal austerity, budgetary constraints, cost containment and cuts in education. Two paradoxes need to be highlighted. First, while the macro-economic policy supports vigorous human resource development to ensure apparent economic expansion, the state's commitment to pay for required investments has not been there. Much of the costs of education are passed on to parents and students. Secondly, policy in South Africa sees the education and training system as a vehicle to improve productivity of the workforce and hence the competitiveness of the South African economy, while simultaneously providing rhetorical support for redistribution and redressing historical imbalances. It has been shown elsewhere that these two goals do not necessarily complement each other. (Samson and Vally 1996).

It is now widely acknowledged that the GEAR strategy has, despite its name, failed in terms of sufficient economic growth, the creation of quality jobs and redistribution towards the poor. The government has presided over an economy in which thousands of jobs have been lost, growth has been negligible and rigid policies have proven inappropriate in the face of South Africa's structural problems. Importantly, the failure of GEAR was predicted by labour from the start, as it was immediately apparent that the strategy was intended for narrow financial stabilisation purposes only.

FURTHER EDUCATION AND TRAINING (FET): SKILLS DEVELOPMENT

The uncritical acceptance of human capital theory that there is a direct relationship between education and the economy is most pronounced in the FET and Skills Development policies. These must be read in conjunction with the Skills Development Act, which aims to establish a system to control and direct the provision of education and training and to guide the implementation of the National Qualifications Framework within the economic sphere. These areas are seen to be crucial to the new information or "knowledge" economy.

Despite the marriage of human capital theory assumptions with notions of redress in South Africa's FET policy, there is a clear danger that individual and institutional redress might be undermined. The financial "allocation by means of competitive bidding" while simultaneously emphasizing "demand-side, rather than supply-side" programmes in order to "re-orient providers to the market and to the needs of the learners" might be driven by the needs of the marketplace and not by the needs of learners or the communities in which they live (DoE 1998). It must be remembered that in South Africa private providers have greater capacity to engage in competitive bidding and are only likely to offer training to those learners who have the ability to pay. There is a danger that the urgency for globally competitive skills will allow employers and macro-economic policies to determine the content of the curriculum and what is valued as knowledge.

While we are, for various reasons, critical of the narrow utilitarian purposes and technicist views of human capital theory and its attendant deficit, we are not arguing that education and training has no role to play in economic development. Rather, the motivation for education and training "must come from an approach to economic and social development which recognizes the inter-relatedness of society and the economy where human values – not human capital – predominate" (Walters 1997). Education and training cannot be the panacea for economic performance, and it certainly should not be used to conceal the intrinsic weakness of the economic structure and unequal ways in which employment is distributed.

Education and training strategies need to confront a number of critical issues. Firstly, a nation's competitive advantage in the global economy is often based on workers' disadvantage. The kind of training which would foster more democratic forms of work organisation and address developmental issues will not necessarily be the same as that which would increase competitiveness. Secondly, the concept of "social development" is not adequately explained in the education and training discourse. Where it is referred to, it is linked to "economic growth." This fits into the "trickle-down" macro-economic view that growth leads automatically to increased well being of the population. This notion prioritizes skills, which boost productivity and competitiveness, but undervalues or neglects those developmental skills necessary to sustain significant numbers of people outside the formal economy. These are the very skills, which make the country not only materially but also culturally prosperous. It is questionable whether industry-led training will adequately address this issue. It has been suggested that skills can be developed in a variety of environments and that other training programmes should co-exist with apprenticeships (NEDLAC 1998). Also, trainees are paid well below prevailing industry rates. Companies might well be prepared to support school leavers and young workers while they go through apprenticeships, but once they qualify and are entitled to higher wages, they are likely to be retrenched.

THE RATIONALISATION OF TEACHERS

The policy of rationalization (or redistribution) of teachers was initially justified on the grounds of achieving equity through equalizing pupil: teacher ratios by redeploying teachers from areas of "oversupply" to areas of "undersupply" within and between provinces. The policy was supported by World Bank research, which selectively used international comparisons to justify arguments for "optimum" class sizes and expenditure on educators, "Although learning is enhanced in classes smaller than 25 pupils," the research concluded, "there is very little difference in learning outcomes in classes between 25 and 40 pupils. When there are over 40 pupils per classroom, however, achievement fails. We think it is reasonable to consider providing classroom space in all primary schools on the basis of 40:1 and in all secondary school classrooms on the basis of 35:1" (World Bank 1995).

The World Bank research on class size has been found to be highly problematic by a number of analysts on several counts. First, the model used by the World Bank was based on a simple input-output mechanism, which denies complex processes of teaching and learning, especially in developing countries. Moreover, it failed to take into consideration the difficulties in implementing the new pedagogies and instructional methods brought about with the new national curriculum. Second, the research neglected to consider the teaching context in South Africa and assumptions around what constitutes "achievement." Class size ended up as the instrument for budgetary control at the exclusion of educational considerations.

It is also worth noting that government policies on teacher distribution hinged on some very questionable Department of Education (DOE) assumptions behind personnel costs. Teacher rationalization was influenced by the recommendations of an international consultant from the World Bank who extrapolated that on the basis of educator costs as a proportion of GDP in ten countries, the salaries of South African educators were higher than can be justified in terms of age, level of educators and other labour market forces (Crouch 1997). Unfortunately, Crouch's data reflected educator costs between 1979 and 1986 and did not include material from South Africa in the ten countries examined. Such data comparisons were dangerously misleading as the educator costs to GDP changed significantly in South Africa, especially over the last decade following the end of apartheid. To argue that we should lower education costs as a proportion of GDP, as Crouch does, without replicating increases in living standards and per capita income of richer countries, offers us a plan that simply neglects the objective conditions facing developing countries such as South Africa.

Two studies that have contested this kind of reasoning have shown that, far from achieving the stated goals of equity and redress, the policy has in fact resulted in a limited redistribution of teachers, the departure of many experienced educators from the public system, greater financial expenditure than was anticipated, job insecurity, significant opposition, and low morale amongst teachers (Chisholm *et al* 1999, Vally and Tleane, 2001). These researchers argue that the primary cause for the failure of this policy is based on the fact the Department of Education allowed budgetary constraints and fiscal austerity measures to shape its equity impulses. Another critic commented " ... policy conclusions about class size is essentially a decision based on economic reasoning which directly counters educational commonsense. Any practicing teacher knows intuitively that teaching 25 children versus teaching 40 children makes completely different demands of pedagogy, management, assessment, curriculum planning, guidance, support, parent relations, etc., especially in the context of a developing country. It is little comfort to such a teacher citing research that claims, "class size makes little difference to achievement" (Jansen 1998). This policy, together with the closing of teacher training colleges, the HIV/AIDS pandemic and the lack of financial support for prospective teachers, has led to a critical shortage of teachers. Annually, the attrition rate for teachers is 21,000 and only 5,000 students qualify as teachers. The latest data show that 5% of teachers are older than 55 years and are about to retire. The HIV prevalence rate is 12.7%, peaking at 21.4% for teachers in the age group 25-34.

THE FUNDING OF SCHOOLS: MIDDLE CLASS MANDATORY FEE CLUSTERING OPTION

Despite a long and complicated process of local consultations, various White Papers and reports, the final funding model for public schools was determined at the behest of international consultants employed by the Department of Education. These consultants (Christopher Colclough and Louis Crouch) recommended the institution of user fees or as it was called the Middle Class Mandatory Fee Clustering Option (Mokgalane and Vally 1996). For these consultants a decline in funding for previously privileged schools would "propel middle-class parents out of the public school sector and into the independent school sector. Among those departing would be many opinion-formers and decision-makers whose influence in favour of sustained or enhanced public funding for public education would consequently diminish" (*Ibid*). To prevent this exodus of middle-class parents the consultants proposed raising resources through user fees from parents who were willing to pay to maintain school quality beyond what would be affordable from the provincial education departments' allocation.

Although the option did not provide convincing answers to a number of problems that emerge in terms of its own assumptions, it was nonetheless adopted. Questions raised included, what will prevent fee-paying parents from moving their children from schools with a preponderance of non fee-paying parents to better-endowed schools within the public school system? The corollary to this was that fee-paying parents might wish to prevent the enrolment of poorer parents who will be exempt from fees, in order to protect the revenue-raising power of their school community and bar "free riders" from enjoying facilities to which they did not contribute.

Despite an overall increase in funding to education, with hindsight it is quite clear that this policy has widened inequality. Schooling is differentiated less by "race" than by class as a result of the user-fees model and market competition between schools. The stratification of schooling in South Africa is similar to patterns of schooling at a global level. For example, the Department of Education's School Register of Needs Survey (2001) estimated that 27% of schools have no running water, 43% have no electricity, and 80% have no libraries. Only about 8,000 out of over 27,000 schools in South Africa have flush sewer toilets while close to 12,300 schools use pit latrines and 2,500 schools have no toilets at all. Even in schools that have toilets, 15.5% are not in working order. Schools requiring additional classrooms number over 10,700.

The evidence suggests that the hope that money saved by the state through the imposition of mandatory fees, which could be deployed for developmental and redress purposes, has not come to fruition. While the National Norms and Standards for School Funding placed emphasis on giving the poorest public schools and those in bad physical condition a larger resource allocation than relatively richer schools, it has not significantly reduced inequalities. This was primarily because it only applied to non-personnel costs which account for 10% or less of provincial education budgets, and in many provinces these have been declining.

Furthermore, the state seems to be shedding its responsibility for the provision of education and transferring it to school governing bodies. The Amendment to the Education Laws Act (1998), which allows governing bodies to employ additional teachers with their own financial resources, will permit further discrepancies between schools and lead to the growth of a labour market in teachers (DoE 1998). Clearly, the labour market involving the purchase of teachers has already gained momentum as the state is determined to reduce personnel expenditure while teacher shortages become more severe. This is a result of the pandemic and previous rationalization policies that were discussed earlier. The Department of Education Needs Survey also revealed that the number of state-paid educators has decreased dramatically by 23,642 while School Governing Body paid educators have increased by 19,000. More affluent schools will be able to choose the most experienced and skilled teachers to the disadvantage of those schools, which have less to offer. Parents on these bodies view their role as co-opted fund-raisers, carrying out provincial and national level instructions, and not as decision makers in education matters.

CURRICULUM 2005: AN OUTCOMES-BASED APPROACH

Much has been written on the influence of Australia, New Zealand and other countries' curriculum models on South Africa's Curriculum 2005 (C2005), particularly it's emphasis on outcomes-based education or OBE. As in most countries around the world, the introduction of OBE has brought with it much controversy and resistance in South Africa. The implementation of OBE in South African schools in 1998 marked a dramatic departure from earlier policy proposals, displacing initiatives such as "peoples education" that had currency with the democratic movement up through the early 1990s.

The introduction of C2005 in South Africa can be mapped to the global rise of competency debates with its emphasis on data-driven, evidence-based accountability measures of educational quality. In many ways it served to reinforce an elaborate global educational monitoring system that is currently being put in place to hold schools and teachers accountable for delivering "quality schools" with "high achievement" regardless of public investiture in education and governmental services to address broad social inequalities. Steiner-Khamsi, *et al* (2005) describe the international resonance of OBE as "signposts of a new neo-liberal era in education reform that epitomized the language of public accountability, effectiveness and market regulation" (2005; 221).

The emphasis of OBE on skills-orientated mastery of pre-determined benchmarks had wide appeal for the goals of integrating education in training in South Africa and elsewhere. Reflecting this global skills-orientation, South African policymakers borrowed broad vocational and occupational outcomes-based frameworks in Australia and the United States (See for instance Spreen, 2004; Jansen, 1999). C2005 mirrored the curriculum statements and the organization of learning areas promoted in Ontario's *Common Curriculum* (developed a number of years ago by the provincial Ministry of Education). It also established accreditation schemes for transfer of credits based on Scotland's vocational and technical standards and created a version of a National Qualifications Framework that relied heavily on the New Zealand qualification frameworks.

While an argument can be made for borrowing from other countries, much of the transference of the new curriculum was selective and from countries very different from South Africa. Countries such as Brazil, where the social dynamics and inequalities are similar to South Africa, were ignored. For example, the curriculum model employed by Paulo Friere, while he was the secretary of education for the Workers' Party administration in the Brazilian city of Sao Paulo, had much to offer and would have accommodated much of the present criticisms leveled at Curriculum 2005 (Torres 1994). Unlike the top-down imposition of policy in South Africa, in Sao Paulo, teachers played a critical role in curriculum reform and curriculum became the centerpiece for a strategy of emancipation. Brazilian educational reforms also involved the active participation of the community at large and the contribution of social movements; they respected the specific dynamics in each school; they used the Freirean methodology of action-reflection in the curriculum; and they included a model of continuing teacher training, with a critical analysis of the curriculum in practice. By contrast, in South Africa, the mass democratic movement was marginalized from the education policy and school reform process. However, in the next section we will see how the historical legacy of the mass democratic movement has become an important asset to contemporary social movements in South Africa, which are leading to vibrant forms of resistance to neo-liberalism.

NEW SOCIAL MOVEMENTS AND RESISTANCE TO NEO-LIBERALISM IN EDUCATION

Today new social movements in South Africa are challenging a wide range of neoliberal reforms. These groups have evolved from the earlier mass democratic movement with the direct benefit of inheriting its organizational capacity and grassroots linkages across a broad range of communities. As a result, new social movements have the ability to mobilize groups in all parts of the country and directly connect to local community-based organizations. These organizations are mostly those outside formal political or governmental institutions and focus on a variety of interrelated issues – poverty, health, education, land rights, and municipal issues.

This resurgence of "popular" movements to broad-based social movements (which are aligned with other global movements) has today evolved into a responsive form of local mobilization against many neoliberal governmental policies in South Africa. For example, the lack of public educational provision has prompted the Education Rights Project (ERP), together with activists from various civil society organizations, to insist on "the right to basic education and adult education" for those from working class communities – a right, which they argue, is at present "no more than a mere constitutional declaration" (Vally 2002:18). The ERP works closely with several social movements and campaigns on issues that include the cost of education infrastructure and facilities, sexual harassment and violence, farm schooling and adult basic education. Since its formation in 2001, the project has held education rights workshops in close to two hundred communities in all provinces of the country and has assisted with numerous cases involving the violation of the legal rights of learners and parents. (ERP Narrative Reports, 2001-2004). It also holds youth camps, seminars on the political economy of education for learners, and student leadership courses together with non-governmental groups and social movements. Students and unemployed youth linked to the ERP have also formed drama groups inspired by the Brazilian dramatist Augusto Boal.

The ERP's participatory research initiatives with emerging social movements and community organisations is a form of social accountability. It asserts the need for civil society to have access to collective self-knowledge, independent of government, in order to hold the state to account for its policies. It is used as a social check on the state's "numbers" and "statistics", which are forwarded by state functionaries as "official justification" for its policies, and in this instance, the right to education. This critical research, according to Kincheloe and McLaren, "becomes a transformative endeavour unembarrassed by the label 'political' and unafraid to consummate a relationship with an emancipatory consciousness." (1998:264) Those in the ERP initiative see their research as "the first step towards forms of political action that can address the injustices found in the field site or constructed in the very act of research itself." (Ibid)

Alongside the cold statistical data on schools fees, transport, feeding schemes, child labour, infrastructure and facilities, the ERP also collects very human testimonies detailing the views and experiences of learners, teachers and community activists about their local schools. The troubles and struggles of individuals and communities to educate their young in very trying conditions and make the hard-won constitutional right to education a reality are vividly portrayed in these testimonies. At the same time, a number of communities are in the process of collecting data on basic issues such as the amount of school fees charged, cost of uniforms, books, transport, provision of meals in schools, household incomes and violations of their rights because of the inability to pay school fees (Spreen and Vally, 2006). These voices help us take a step back to understand the failures of policy, as Apple and Beane (1999) suggest, outside its "glossy political rhetoric" and place them in the gripping "details of everyday life."

Although many of the social movements are not always able to provide sophisticated alternatives to the status quo, it is precisely the constituencies they represent that have brought about the most significant changes in this country. Popular energies, which once sustained the powerful pre-1994 education social movements, are again resurgent. These new social movements have not only established continuity with past struggles but they have also shed the disarming and misplaced hope that formal political and constitutional change is sufficient to realise socio-economic rights and democratic citizenship.

CONCLUSION

As a response to the pressures of globalisation, education in South Africa is increasingly being focused on the production of skilled workers to bolster the country's competitive edge within an international capitalist economy. The articulation of this goal with present macro-economic imperatives (such as fiscal austerity measures and the reliance on market mechanisms) has resulted in the increased commodification of education and its transformation into a service rather than a right or a common good. As a consequence, the social justice hopes for the country's schools are being sacrificed. We have no doubt that many of the post-1994 functionaries staffing the provincial and national education departments in South Africa are well intentioned and have produced some innovative policies. But they cannot escape the impossibility of implementing genuine social development initiatives within an export oriented and market dependent macro-economic framework. This is a framework that is inimical to the social justice policies propounded in South Africa's formal policy texts. For us a *sine qua non* for meeting the goals of genuine transformation and redistribution is a political struggle in direct opposition to the present macro-economic strategy.

Beyond this, we concur with Henry *et al* (1999) that at the global level we can increasingly imagine global alliances between social groups battered by the vagaries of the global market. In fact, globalisation itself, through new technologies and the global flow of ideas and information, provides opportunities "to find a common language with which to confront the various destructive aspects of global capitalism." (*Ibid*) We need more globalisation from below through unions, progressive education networks and other global alliances in order to produce alternative arguments through what Henry *et al* call "a new regime of thinkability." We need to build on a wide body of international research into the shifting forms of neo-liberalism within our schools and our societies at the same time as we build on the popular resistance to the implementation of these forms – in finance, in governance and in curriculum.

We agree with Michael Apple's (1999) conclusion that "it would be an act of utter foolishness to give capitalism a free ride, to not name it for what it is and what it does. And no amount of theoretical elegance must allow us to distance ourselves from this. We must never excuse as somehow necessary or inevitable the suffering that its inequalities, exploitations, and alienations not only allow, but constantly produce."

BIBLIOGRAPHY

Apple, M (1999) *Power, Meaning and Identity*, Peter Lang.

Apple, M and Beanne J (eds) (1999) *Democratic Schools: Lessons from the Chalk Face*. Open University Press: London.

Blackmore, J (1999) "Localization/globalization and the midwife state: strategic dilemmas for state feminism in education?" *Journal of Education Policy*, vol.14, no.1

Bond, P (2006) "Lack of service delivery is turning poor settlements into hotbeds of activism" in *Sunday Independent*, 29th January.

Carrim, N (1998), *An Analysis of Curriculum Development and Curriculum Materials in Regard to Human Rights, Democracy and Citizenship Education in Contemporary South Africa*, CIES World Congress, Cape Town, 12-17 July.

Chisholm, L (1997), "The Restructuring of South African Education and Training in a Comparative context in Kallaway, P, *Education After Apartheid*, UCT Press, 1997.

Chisholm, L and Fuller, B (1996), "Remember People's Education? Shifting Alliance, State Building and South Africa's Narrowing Policy Agenda", *Journal of Education Policy*, vol.11, no.6.

Chisholm, L, Soudien, C, Vally, S, Gilmour, D (1999) "Structural Adjustment and Teachers in South Africa, *Journal of Education Policy*, vol.13, no.3, July.

Christie, P (1997) "Global Trends in Local Contexts: a South African perspective on competence debates, *Discourse: studies in the cultural politics of education*, vol.18, no.1

Community Constituency submission to NEDLAC, June 1998. Unpublished mimeo.

Crouch, L (1997), *Personnel Costs in South African Education: No Easy Solutions*, Department of Education/Education Foundation, December.

Dale, R (1999), "Specifying globalization effects on national policy: a focus on the mechanisms," *Journal of Education Policy*, vol.14, no.1.

Department of Education (1998) *Amendment to the Education Laws Act*, Pretoria.

Department of Education (1998), *Green Paper on Further Education and Training*, Pretoria.

Department of Education (2001) *School Register of Needs Survey*, Pretoria.

ERP Narrative Reports (2001-2004). Unpublished.

Henry, M, Lingard, B, Rizvi, F and Taylor, S (1999), "Working with/against globalisation in education", *Journal of Education Policy*, vol.14, no.1.

Jansen, J (1998) "How To Make Teachers Disappear: International Research and the Education Policies of Developing Countries," Unpublished, July.

Walter, S (1997) *Globalisation, Adult Education and Training*, Zed Books.

Kincheloe, J.L and McLaren, P. (1998) "Rethinking Critical Theory and Quantitative Research." In eds N. Denzin and S. Lincoln *The Landscape of Qualitative Research Theories and Issues*. Sage: Thousand Oaks.

Marginson, S (1999) "After globalization: emerging politics of education", *Journal of Education Policy*, vol.14, no.1, January-February.

Mkhatshwa, S, (1999) Opening Address, Southern African Comparative and History of Education Society, (SACHES), Roodepoort, 30 September, 1999.

Mokgalane, E and Vally, S (1996), "Between Vision and Practice: Policy Processes and Implementation," *Quarterly Review of Education and Training*, March.

Motala, S and Vally, S (2002) "From People's Education to Tirisano" in Kallaway, P(ed) The History of Education Under Apartheid, Peter Lang, London.

Samson, M and Vally, S (1996) "Snakes and Ladders: The Promise and Potential Pitfalls of the National Qualifications Framework (NQF)," *South African Labour Bulletin*, vol.2, no.4.

Spreen, C (2004) "Appropriating Borrowed Policies: outcomes-based education in South Africa," in G. Steiner-Khamsi (ed.) *The Global Politics of Educational Borrowing and Lending*. New York: Teachers College Press.

Spreen, C and Vally, S (forthcoming March 2006), "Education Rights, Education Policies and Inequality in South Africa", *International Journal of Education and Development.*

Steiner-Khamsi, G, Silova, I and Johnson, E (forthcoming 2006) "Neoliberalism liberally applied. Educational policy borrowing in Central Asia" (forthcoming).

Torres, C (1994), "Paulo Freire as Secretary of Education in the Municipality of Sao Paulo, *Comparative Education Review*, vol.38, no.2.

Vally, S and Tleane, C (2001) "Teacher Rationalisation and the Quest for Social Justice in Education" in Pampallis, J and Motala, E (eds) *Education and Equity: The Impact of State Policies on South African Education*, Ashgate Publishers, London.

Vally, S (2002) "Human Rights, Neo-liberalism and Education", *Quarterly Review of Education and Training*, December.

World Bank Southern Africa Department (1995), South Africa Education Sector: Strategic Issues and Policy Options, Washington.

NOTES

[1] According to a United Nations Development Programme report released in May 2004, nearly 22 million South Africans (48,5 % of the population) fell below the poverty line – R354 a month – compared to 20,2 million or 51% in 1995. The UNDP's Human Development Index ranks South Africa 120th out of 177 countries. The report also captures the increasing inequality in South Africa-the richest 10% had a 44.7% share of total income and consumption while the poorest 10% had only 1.4%. Statistics SA, a statutory body, also noted that the rate of unemployment soared from 16% in 1995 to almost 30% in 2000. Survival strategies such as employment in precarious and poorly paid work in the informal sector are not considered in these unemployment statistics. The addition of such categories would increase the unemployment figures to catastrophic levels. Although the ruling party has claimed that government spending on welfare and service subsidies has boosted the effective incomes of the poor and ameliorated poverty, the UNDP report found that 65% of households are still deprived of access to at least one basic social service. Although the government document "Toward a Ten Year Review" lists the progress made

in housing, electrification and housing since 1994, it is silent about the number of those who have defaulted on their home loans and those who have suffered disconnections as a result of failure to pay the user fees for these utilities

[2] These include the Anti-Privatisation Forum, the Landless People's Movement, the Anti-Eviction Campaign, the Abahlali Base Mjondolo and the Concerned Citizen's Forum.

Creating Schools with a New Education of Hope

THE KOREAN TEACHERS AND EDUCATION WORKERS UNION

The Korean Teachers and Education Workers Union (Chunkyojo) launched a "School Innovation Campaign" in 2005. Led by the School Innovation Team, this campaign inherits the spirit of Chamgyoyook, which focuses on enhancing teaching and learning in Korea. Our goal is to establish a "new school for the 21st century" that provides quality public education.

Education in Korea faces a serious challenge: business and government are pushing for market-oriented changes in public education. These changes have tarnished the public features of education, and the "education gap" between social classes and regions is widening. As neo-liberal policies are emphasized, students are forced to vie for higher test scores and competitiveness is prevalent among teachers and schools. Neo-liberal ideas that emphasize economic efficiency and profit while ignoring education philosophy and principals are threatening to determine the future of Korean education.

Chunkyojo has been designing strategies that oppose government-imposed neoliberal education measures, and has created a plan that guarantees quality public education by "building democratic school communities run by teachers, students and parents." It also encourages teachers' spontaneous efforts to innovate curriculum and teaching methods.

The most important feature of our campaign is its determination to change education not through bureaucratic policies, but through individual teachers' passion and spontaneity. We firmly believe that teach-

ers are capable of taking the helm of a new education, and that all schools in Korea will be completely reborn for the 21st century.

Lee, Dong-jin

I

WHY SCHOOL INNOVATION? WHY A NEW EDUCATION?

Changing Times and Societal Demands

It can be said that education in South Korea faces a comprehensive crisis. The Ministry of Education and Human Resources Development has proven incapable of presenting a vision or blueprint for innovation. At the same time, parents and students' distrust of school-based education continues to deepen. Their distress increasingly manifests itself in denunciations of and attacks against teachers. The "education problem," its various components so intricately intertwined with external factors, cannot be resolved with any single measure, or with partial ameliorative or palliative efforts.

The development and spread of the Internet and information technology – reflecting an accelerated transition to a "knowledge society" – is pressing education for qualitative change. It calls for a change in the education system, from a system whose structure is characteristic of an industrial society, to a system that corresponds to an information and knowledge-based society. This social change calls for a re-orientation of the status and role of school-based education that recognizes the importance of life-long learning.

There is a growing public consciousness that education-related decision-making cannot be monopolized by the Ministry of Education, Offices of Education, or teachers. This is accompanied by a greater demand of parents to participate in the decisions that affect education, and the growing voice for students' right to learn. These changes are paralleled by criticism that school-based education is unable to foster the growth and development of the personalities and creativities of individual students. All these factors have prompted an "exodus" where parents, unwilling to accept the limitations and rigidity of the school system, opt for "alternative" schools for their children. There is also a growing movement for teachers to be evaluated by parents. At the same time, the increased autonomy of regional governments in administrative affairs has allowed local governments and councils opportunities to make their own policy interventions in school-related matters.

In various countries, including the "educationally-advanced" countries of northern Europe, proposals and discussions for "education for the future," "sustainable education," etc. are being presented as part of efforts to develop new education systems to meet the demands of the 21st century. These discussions include a fundamental re-thinking of the meaning of education, and the development of new concepts of education. These extend to, and provide foundations for, efforts to innovate school systems, review the function of schools and the roles of teachers, and the development of new curricula and pedagogies. These efforts have been undertaken by various organizations, and in many cases governments, teachers' organizations, and individual teachers are working together.

Teachers and other experts are called upon to present appropriate responses to present demands for change and innovation. This needs to start with a comprehensive overhaul of a feudalistic education system that has prevailed since the days of the Japanese colonial domination, towards a participatory and democratic system for the 21st century. This new system must foster individual personality and creativity and be based on respect for the environment and life.

Government's education policies: contradictions and limitations

The public education system of South Korea began as a mechanism of colonial domination by Japanese imperialist forces. Under the militaristic imperative of the latter days of its colonial domination, the education system became rigidly monolithic and authoritarian. Following liberation, in the course of the rule of the U.S. military government, which prevailed in South Korea for the first three years of the post-liberation period and throughout the 1950s, the education system remained unchanged from that which was established by the Japanese colonial government. Colonial structures and practices were maintained, and key personnel who had served under Japanese rule were entrenched in the system. One change that came about was the grafting of certain aspects of the American education system, including its basic structure and divisions. Under the government of president Rhee Syngman, Japanese collaborators succeeded in maintaining their positions. They adopted American education policies and institutions indiscriminately, and are responsible for the current general design of the education system.

During the military dictatorships, from the Park Chung-hee regime to that of Roh Tae-woo, authoritarianism, bureaucratism, and a monolithic militaristic culture of control became the flesh and bone of education administration. The administration of schools was determined by the guidance and directives of the Education Ministry and Regional Offices of Education; heads of schools could never become the focal points of school communities, but were forced to function as the last apparatchik in the chain of command emanating from the Regional Office of Education. The Park Chung-hee regime concentrated on expanding school-based education as a means to develop and secure the "manpower" required for economic development. The regime was not interested in investing in qualitative development, which resulted in over-crowded classes and a mushrooming of large schools. This sprouted the seeds of long-lasting contradictions in the education system in South Korea.

Since the first-ever civilian government of president Kim Young-sam, the government's education ministries have repeatedly initiated various so-called reform policies. The result, however, has always been inappropriate policy packages which lacked depth of thinking and a detailed understanding of the school realities. They were pursued in "top-down" fashion, giving rise to tension and conflicts among the different group of education practitioners. They were always accompanied by an increased workload, and generated obstacles and difficulties for education activities at the school level. Failures that were repeated routinely with changes in government have contributed to the lack of confidence in school-based education, aggravating the "reform-fatigue" suffered by the various groups of education providers and receivers.

The basic orientation of education policy, since the days of the first civilian government, has been the characterization of education as a service. With education defined as a service, policy debates have been driven by concerns for "consumer-orientation" and "efficiency and competitiveness." The underlying doctrine has been that education needs to be governed by the principles of a market economy. In more than 10 years of market-oriented education reforms, a knowledge-dominant education aimed at reflecting an information society has ignored the importance and philosophy of a "holistic" human education. At the same time, it has brought about an unravelling of community-spirited cooperation, initiative and self-reliance for various actors in education. The result has been a loss of the school's potential to function as an education community devoted to fostering holistic human growth.

School-based education in South Korea continues to be determined by the contradictions and shortcomings introduced and consolidated by colonial domination and military dictatorship. This includes top-down commandist bureaucratism, authoritarianism, monolithic militaristic culture, centralized-and-concentrated administration, and teachers who have been acclimatized to this structure. These traits have been the shackles that restrain efforts toward genuine democracy. "Guidelines" or "directives" of the education ministry or regional education offices are implemented in every area in every school, while each school is governed by the whims of the headmaster. While there has been some progress in procedural democracy in the course of the three terms of civilian government since the early 1990s, the traditional framework of both education administration and school administration has not changed in its essence.

The realities and challenges of the teacher union movement

The trade union of teachers Chunkyojo (Korean Teachers and Education Workers Union) considers national community, democratic society, and humanization the three pillars of education and endeavours to practice cham-education (true-education), which seeks to advance these values. The work of the teachers trade union movement has focused on criticising the mistaken and foolhardy policies of the government and, when necessary, resisting them by mobilizing its members. At the same time, it has devoted itself to addressing major education-related concerns through collective bargaining with the education ministry. In doing so, the teachers' trade union movement has neglected somewhat the work of proposing and engaging in discussions about the goals and visions of education with the wider education community, civil society, organised peoples movements, and political movements. The teachers' union has, in short, failed to initiate, generate, and empower a society-wide debate or consensus on education.

The recent series of misdeeds and acts of corruption involving school teachers, including misconduct related to university entry procedures and student school records, have greatly damaged confidence in and authority of teachers, bringing people's distrust of teachers and schools to a new, critical, level. The teachers union is beginning to be perceived by many, not as a movement of teachers devoted to the ideals of cham-education with passion for genuine education, but as an "interest group," formed to defend its own interests. Chunkyojo itself suffers from various "ailments," such as the declining rate of new membership and the weakening of a passion to achieve cham-education. It is affected by various pressures arising from within and without the union.

Education personnel, especially teachers, have recently been portrayed by a conservative establishment as a narrow-minded and indifferent group holding onto its vested interests and old antiquated paradigms. This has given the initiative to those who support a market-oriented education. Teacher evaluation, the disclosure of school information, autonomy for local administrations, and the regional consolidation of education jurisdictions are proceeding with great speed, while cyber-home-learning, e-learning, and u-learning have become the central tenets of education policy direction. If the teachers union is "bogged down" in resisting these reform initiatives, community-oriented education reform may never see the light of the day.

Chunkyojo has prepared a "Proposal for Public Education Reorganisation" aimed at a comprehensive overhaul of the public education system. It has initiated discussions for a new framework for public education, including the system of school levels. However, Chunkyojo was not able to use the "Proposal for Public Education Reorganisation" as a platform for a campaign to empower teachers, parents and students, and civil society as a whole, or to become agents for action and alternative practice.

Institutional reforms, such as a legislative framework for school autonomy and the election of school principals, which need to be undertaken at the state level, are important pre-conditions for innovation of the school system. However, in order for laws and institutions to bring about the realization of the objectives underlying them, there is a need for people who are empowered and committed to make use of the rights guaranteed by such institutional instruments. Herein lies the need to organize various education actors – teachers, parents, students and others – to become active agents in efforts to bring about changes in legislation and institutions. Such a two-pronged effort is vital for genuine change.

Today, there is an urgent need to develop specific demands and proposals for institutional reform, rooted in a structured and long-term understanding and vision. There is a parallel need to empower education actors as agents for change. This calls for civil society movements, community movements, and social movements to become forces for reform. The effort requires an integrated strategy and grassroots-based action plan. Teachers, especially members of Chunkyojo, are central to efforts for innovation, and parents, students, and communities need to be empowered as agents for innovation.

Chunkyojo needs to present to the public in general a vision of community-oriented education reform with a programme that will be accepted as feasible, and to build society-wide consensus and support. Members of Chunkyojo in each school need to organize a school innovation ("new school") campaign with all concerned education actors, to be combined with a society-wide campaign to press the government to produce a comprehensive reform policy that will overhaul the school system. The teachers union movement needs to go beyond the current campaigns and struggles to resist foolhardy and wrong-headed government policies; it needs to respond positively to the demands of changing times and social demands, and be in a position to lead the process of change.

II

"NEW EDUCATION MOVEMENT" FOR A FUTURE OF HOPE

We must work to liberate the school from antiquated structures and practices, to make it a place where education for hope and the future is undertaken, as a part of a larger effort to rebuild society as a life community for all peoples. The "New Education Movement" will need to be both an education reform movement and social reform movement, in which Chunkyojo takes the lead, with teachers, parents, and students empowered as agents for change, supported by wider civil society movements. It will need to be an "offensive" effort to overcome neoliberalism, which has been destroying the community with its insistence on competitiveness and efficiency. It will need to be a movement that changes the school and education, and in doing so, the society-world itself.

The "New Education Movement" must be a movement to overcome the market fundamentalism that destroys the community with its drive for efficiency and competitiveness; it must be a movement to remake the school as a place of education-community where people learn and practice sharing and co-existence. The "New Education Movement" must be an effort to dismantle the "law of jungle" which drives the majority of people into impoverishment and to the sidelines in the course of victories for a few winners. It must be a movement to rebuild a genuine community where the life and rights of every individual person are respected and valued.

The goal of building a community of sharing and co-existence, with a new education founded on the values of sustainable ecology and environments requires, for its realization, an active education community rooted in classrooms, schools, and local communities. This calls for teachers, students, parents and local communities to develop a shared vision for school innovation. It also calls for energetic actions and activities and broad coalitions, alliances, and networks to translate the vision into reality. Community-oriented education reform will only be possible when there is a groundswell of grassroots education movements in which various education actors and civil society come together at the location of the school (e.g., local government ordinance for school lunch campaigns).

Once a consensus is created within and without the union for a programme of "creating new schools for a future of hope," and discussions have taken place at each school for specific plans and actions for innovation, broader civil society movements, community movements, and the people's movement as a whole will begin to adopt school innovation as their own agenda, laying the ground for cooperation, joint campaigns, and solidarity. This will create momentum for Chunkyojo to engage political parties and the government directly, to present and demand a set of bold policy initiatives to create a new school system for the 21st century.

Once the movement, generated by actors at each school, spreads to become a broader movement rooted in local communities, school and education innovation can become a central issue in various public elections, such as the nation-wide local elections in 2006, the local education administration elections, and the presidential election in 2007. This will enable school reform actors to call on the various political parties to respond to the vision and policies for innovation generated by the movement.

III

INDICATORS OF SCHOOL INNOVATION: WHAT KIND OF SCHOOL IS NEEDED FOR A 21ST CENTURY SOUTH KOREA?

An image of the new school for 21st century South Korea:

- School as a joyful living-space, cultivating life, celebrating a diverse student culture;
- School that respects students' integrity and rights, and fosters students personalities and creative abilities;
- School that provides a living experience of a community life of co-existence and sharing.

What kind of education is needed for 21st century South Korean schools?

- A holistic education facilitating harmonious and balanced; development of knowledge, virtue, and body;
- Education where students learn to live together with neighbours in community;
- Education where students learn to respect life, co-existence with nature, and the value of work;
- Education oriented to the co-existence of peoples of different nations, international cooperation and world peace.

The basic principles in school operation:

- School operates on the basis of consensus of all its constituent members, mutual respect, cooperative participation and action;
- School operates on participation and is governed by students, teachers, and parents, rather than on the basis of directives and top-down control;
- School operates on the basis of cooperation between school (teachers), homes (parents), and local community (civil society);
- School where learning focuses on specific needs of students in their community, where teachers are able to work in teams, on the basis of self-reliance and specialities.

IV

TASKS FOR SCHOOL INNOVATION

1. We work first to change the school.

Task 1 – Innovation of the school management system:

- Democratic decision making process: democratic operation of general teachers meetings, level teachers meetings, subject teachers meetings, budget review committees, personnel committees, education planning meetings, school management committees, education activity evaluation meetings;
- Establish a rational operating system: education planning -> budget-making -> transparent execution -> evaluation loop;
- Eradicate bureaucratic authoritarianism: minimize official directives from Regional Offices of Education (which require reply preparation by teachers), reduce non-teaching workload of teachers, end unnecessary events;
- Organisational innovation to emphasise education activities: readjust the activities of the level teachers and subject teachers meetings, the work of division head teachers, the work of administrative division;
- Innovate the division head teacher system: strengthen the role of level teachers division heads, introduce a full-time division head responsible for administrative work, introduce elections for head teachers;
- Empower participation and self-government: democratic communication, mutual respect and cooperation amongst various education actors;
- Democratic participation of parents in school affairs: parent association for different levels, teacher-parent dialogue, participation in school education evaluation;
- Open school in a local community: support for educational activities of local cultural workers, activists, local community organisations.

Task 2 – Innovation of education curricula and education activities:

- Provide and run diverse education curricula for individual schools and regions (experience-learning, special aptitude education, localization);
- Innovate education methodology: project-based teaching, empower cooperative and discussion-based learning, self-initiated study activities;
- Re-organise the school term structure and diversification of the academic calendar: re-examine February term, Spring and Autumn breaks;
- Systematic vocational education programme: job study and experience as a part of vocational guidance;
- Innovate teacher upgrade training system: introduce "teacher study terms," develop cooperation with universities for provision of teachers continued training;
- Abolish various ritualistic (show-window) events and programmes: incorporate important events into the curricula;
- Develop subjective-evaluation to avoid "single correct answer" testing: prepare the conditions;
- Reduce the number of subjects to be completed in each school term, reduce the number of classes per day;
- Autonomy for organization of classes and timetable.

Task 3 – Student self-government, innovation of culture and welfare facilities:

- Guarantee democratic organization and self-reliant activities of student association; representation in School Management Committee;
- Adoption of democratic regulations for student life to protect students personality and human rights;
- Foster and support students self-initiated club activities: innovation of the system of self-development activities;
- Empowering student cultural activities, regularization of school festivals: assignment of teachers specializing in support for student self-government and cultural activities.

- Provision of indoor and outdoor rest facilities, refurbish toilets, washbasins, and other welfare and sanitation facilities;
- Reorganise school lunch system to provide safe, environment-friendly agricultural produce;
- Respect the decisions of the student association and extend maximum support for their activities;
- Guarantee the participation of the leader of student association in School Management Committees as observer and to present opinions.

Task 4 – Innovation of school and education environments: school re-modelling:

- Limit the number of students for each class to less than 30; efforts to make small-size schools;
- Reconfiguration of classrooms focusing on education activities: teacher study room, library, art classroom, science classroom, and other special activities rooms;
- Expand indoor space with sufficient natural light;
- Secure subject classrooms, group study rooms, outdoor classrooms, audio-visual rooms, small theatres, club rooms, etc.;
- Secure sufficient comfort and welfare facilities for students and teachers;
- Create nature-friendly school environments and facilities, such as gardens, forests, ponds, etc.

2. Build the 21st century school on the basis of school self-government.

Task 1 – Legislations for school self-government:

- Establish the legal status, rights, and responsibilities of teachers associations, parents associations, and student associations, and their cooperative relationships;
- Major education activities to be undertaken on the basis of deliberation by self-governing bodies and School Management Committees.

Task 2 – Election of school principal:

- Establish the role and status of school principals as the first among school actors, and focal point in a democratic process of eliciting the wisdom and consensus of all school constituents;
- Establish school principals as teaching principals: require principals to take around seven hours of teaching per week;
- Abolish the vice-principal position and work-evaluation point system: establish democratic school education plan, introduce a comprehensive school evaluation system.

Task 3 – Innovate the regional office of education – transformation into "education support centre":

- Regional offices of education to be transformed into support centre for creative school management and operation: serve as a hub of network of schools;
- Introduce an in-field teacher school inspector system: adopt teachers with proven experience in education activities as school inspectors;
- Regional offices of education need to work to channel and link various human and material resources of communities with schools.

3. Create an education of hope together with local communities.

Task 1 – "Experience-Learn Education Support Centres":

- Thematic experience-learn education centres (environment, vocational exploration, marine life, astronomy, pottery, craft, etc.);
- Develop experience-learn activity programmes linked to school education curricula;
- Develop weekday, week-end, vacation camp activity programmes for different levels;
- Nature study and nature experience programmes utilizing underused schools;
- Assignment of experience-learning special teachers, provision of buses for transportation.

Task 2 – Youth Education Cultural Centres:

- Build new comprehensive youth education and cultural centres or remodel/reorganize existing youth training centres as facilities, which contain a library, gymnasium, swimming pool, cultural centre, and performance theatre;
- Serve as support centres for special activities, sports activities, cultural-arts activities, special aptitude activities education;
- Serve as support centres for education and cultural space and life-long education, especially in view of the five-day work week;
- Coordination between school education and the programmes provided by local youth cultural and welfare facilities;
- Identify local community human resources for school networks within each school district.

Task 3 – Education support for rural and remote areas and low income families:

- Special support for schools in rural and remote areas: a special law for promotion of education in rural and remote areas;
- Expand education welfare for students of low-income families: scholarship support for students of disadvantaged families;
- Promote pre-school education: expand opportunities for pre-school education as public education.

4. Experimental Initiative for Diverse School Models.

- School within school: create two "separate" schools within single large schools, on the basis of year-levels or education plans;
- Public autonomous schools in rural and remote areas: allow diverse experimental education in small public schools in rural and remote areas;
- Small schools in urban areas: experimental "small schools" using cultural or sport facilities in large cities;
- Primary-Middle Combined Schools: experimental operation of combined schools (of 10 school years) in rural and remote areas, incorporating pre-school, primary school, and middle school.

V

ACTION STRATEGY OF SCHOOL INNOVATION

1. Sharing of vision and cases.

- Propose discussion on 21st century school innovation at the conference of union's school chapter representatives: propose teacher-parent discussion at each school;
- Campaign and publicity promotion: organize various promotion and publicity campaigns on issues of school innovation, 21st century school of hope project, utilizing mass media;
- Establish a website: to serve as a online centre for information sharing and exchange for school innovation ;
- Dialogue with local community organizations: explore cooperation, solidarity activities, forum, discussion, etc.;
- Networking between schools and local community through cham-education study groups, small school action groups, etc.

2. Direction of activities for school innovation: campaigns for the self-realisation and development of school actors.

- School innovation campaign: realizing cham-education;
- A campaign to promote macro-level institutional reform to organize a core group of committed actors and to bring about improvement on the basis of the consciousness and actions of various education groups; at the school level, the campaign needs to bring together union members, colleagues, school principal, parents, and students; the school constituent groups need to develop specific innovation tasks and actions suitable to the conditions in individual schools;
- Establish various plans to bring about change, such as: actions to solve specific problems encountered at individual schools, education planning, and school development planning; focusing on improvements in school management, school-based education systems, education curricula, education activities, education environments, education conditions.

- A local, grassroots education-community campaign;

  - The 21st century school needs to communicate and cooperate closely with the local community and draw on the diverse resources of the local community. The new school needs to be a central focus of local communities. The union's local chapters, regional branches, and head office need to be able to resolve local education issues through diverse, solidarity-building activities among education actors and community organizations.

  - Community leaders and activists need to be participate in expanding of student welfare, supporting disadvantaged youth, establishing experience-learning centres, developing youth education and cultural centres, eradicating oversized classes, and opening up education issues in rural and remote areas.

- A campaign for institutional reforms for school innovation;

  - This is a campaign to secure administrative and financial resources needed for school innovation. It directs its activities toward the government and the National Assembly. This campaign needs to be spearheaded by the national office in cooperation and solidarity with various civil society organizations dealing with education issues. It may call for political negotiations.

  - The tasks which need to be addressed by this campaign are: legislation for school self-government, election of school principals, transformation of the regional offices of education into education support centres, innovation of the teacher continuing-training system, and the School Management Committee.

Neo-Liberalism in the Schools of Western Europe

KEN JONES AND NATHALIE DUCEUX

It has become commonplace to claim that governments have no power to halt or inflect the economic forces which shape contemporary societies – they must submit to free market globalisation and to the agenda of the institutions which further its projects. This claim has in Europe a reverse side: while acquiescent in relation to market trends, governments must in other ways be ceaselessly active, reshaping their social systems to respond to new exigencies – creating, in Tony Blair's words, "a competitive basis of physical infrastructure and human skill" and managing the social conflicts attendant upon neo-liberal change.[1] The transformation of education is central to this reshaping, and has accordingly been placed at the centre of the agenda of national governments, and, increasingly, of the European Union itself. No aspect of education systems – from financing to forms of selection, from pedagogy to questions of management – is spared the critical scrutiny of governments committed to market-driven change.

In this chapter, we reflect on the impact of neo-liberal globalisation on the education systems of West European societies,[2] identifying a policy orthodoxy that affects all countries, and owes much to the interaction of the programmes of national governments with the work of international organisations – the European Union, in particular – whose policy repertoire is growing in influence. It was not always thus: the 1957 Treaty of Rome, the founding document of the EEC, made just a single mention of education, in the form of a reference to vocational training.

The Brussels Treaty of 1965, which created a Commission and a Council of Ministers, laid the basis for more extensive work. EEC ministers of education met for the first time in 1971. By 1974, there existed a Community education committee consisting of the permanent representatives of national ministers. In 1976, emerging from this slow consolidation of executive competences, came the first resolution of the European Council, relating to "co-operation in the field of education". It proposed a modest enough programme – research, the collection of statistics, the beginnings of projects aimed at strengthening through educational mobility a conception of European citizenship. These initiatives had an economic aspect; the mobility of labour and the harmonisation of qualifications were among their objectives. But they represented only a small part of an educational project that from the eighties onwards grew considerably in scale and ambition. "Following the Reagan-Thatcher period of the 1980s," write Laval and Weber, "there developed a tendency to view education as an economic tool, at the service of the economy and its competitiveness … and this pulled education towards the centre … of Community policies".[3] In this context, the Single European Act (1986) emphasised the importance of "human resource development." For a period in the late eighties, the early years of the Delors presidency of the Commission, the emphasis on liberalisation and competitiveness was balanced and to some extent concealed by Delors' advocacy of a social Europe in which questions of cohesion and quality of life would be primary. The social model lives on in the rhetoric of the EU (and in the hopes of the European TUC); but in practice the Treaty of Maastricht (1992), and its creation of Monetary Union, a Central Bank, and financial "convergence criteria" for the euro, established a market-driven dynamic at the centre of Europe.

Maastricht underlined the importance of high-quality education to the Community. At the same time, it recognised that the organisation and content of education remained the responsibility of member states. But this latter principle, though still inscribed in the foundational texts of the EU, became increasingly compromised. The Commission's White Papers of the mid-nineties helped diffuse a policy orthodoxy in which the organisation and content of education, as well as its more general purposes, were established as matters for strategic discussion.[4] As neo-liberal principles became hegemonic, so a parallel process of educational convergence occurred. The European Council (Heads of State) meeting in Lisbon in 2000 marked a new stage in the involvement of the EU at a detailed level of education policy. The Council declared that the EU, facing the challenges of globalisation and of a burgeoning knowledge economy, must, by 2010, transform itself into "the most dynamic and competitive knowledge economy in the world."[5] Education systems were placed unequivocally at the centre of the transformation: "never before," according to the Council, "had systems of education and training been recognised as central to economic and social strategy and to the future of the EU."[6] "European policy in the field of education and training," stated the Portuguese Presidency of the Council, "must look beyond the incremental reform of existing systems. It must also take as its objectives the construction of a European educational space of lifelong education and training, and the emergence of a knowledge society."[7] Through the Lisbon discussions, and those of the Council meetings that followed, the governments of the member countries delegated to the Commission the power to settle large-scale questions relating to the orientation of education systems. In the words of the 2001 document *Future Objectives*: "We must certainly preserve the differences in system and structure which reflect the identities of the countries and regions of Europe, but we must equally recognise that our principal objectives, and the results at which we all aim, are remarkably similar ... No member is in a position to accomplish such goals alone. Our societies, like our economies, are today too interdependent to make such an option realistic."[8]

The Lisbon summit licensed the translation of the general terms of knowledge society discourse into concrete policy objectives at a European level. Subsequent Council meetings, in Stockholm (2001) and Barcelona (2002) elaborated this work. At Stockholm, ministers of education decided on three strategic objectives, relating to "quality," "access" and "opening education to the outside world." At Barcelona, these were further refined into thirteen "concrete objectives": "quality" involved, among other things, "developing the competences required for the knowledge society"; "access" emphasised active citizenship, equal opportunity and social cohesion; "the outside world" was translated as "the world of work," with a particular emphasis on developing the "spirit of enterprise."[9] Accompanying this work of definition was a programme of implementation, involving annual European-level reviews of progress made by member states, benchmarked against 16 "quality indicators" developed by the Commission[10]; at the same time the Commission began the work of identifying "new basic competences" and "future objectives of national education systems" in the knowledge society.[11]

A NEW POLICY INSTRUMENT

The turn towards concreteness, target-setting and monitoring took the Commission beyond its previous powers and constitutional authority. Formally, the EU has no legal capacity to intervene in the structure, organisation and content of education in the member states; it needed therefore to make use of a new policy instrument, the Open Method of Co-ordination, a device which took the development of EU education policy to a new level.[12] In the words of the European Presidency (2000) the OMC involves:

- fixing guidelines for the Union combined with specific timetables for achieving the goals which they set in the short, medium and long terms; establishing, where appropriate,
- quantitative and qualitative indicators and benchmarks against the best in the world …;
- translating these European guidelines into national and regional policies by setting specific targets and adopting measures, taking into account national and regional differences;
- periodic monitoring, evaluation and peer review as mutual learning processes. (European Presidency 2000, paragraph 37).

Alexiadou is one of many who argue that "the OMC will radically challenge how education policy is governed in the EU … since member states will no longer enjoy exclusive sovereignty over education policy." She envisages a "complex system of multi-level governance," in which the OMC will be a powerful normative force.[13] The norms to which it works are formally pluralist – "competitiveness," "knowledge based-economy," "sustainable growth," "more and better jobs" and "social cohesion" are all prominent themes. In practice, however, the dominant discourse is "competitiveness"; as Dale puts it, any contradictions between economic and social discourses are likely to be resolved in favour of the former.[14] In this way, the OMC provides governments with a further weapon for use against national traditions that have been shaped, at least in part, by social forces seeking other objectives than economisation. It is in reality, suggests Christian Laval, a "convergence that will not speak its name."[15]

THE ROLE OF THE NATION STATE

EU policy does not, of course, arrive like an invading army, catching the governments of member states by surprise: on the contrary, it provides them with a means of legitimizing and furthering programmes of change to which national élites have long been committed. Nor does the EU substitute for the political work that national states must do to bring about neo-liberal change; defeating opposition, establishing a new educational consensus, translating policies into concrete and complex programmes of reform are tasks that can only be carried through at a national level. In the following section, we consider some of the forms taken by national-level strategies of change. In the limited space available we focus on a single topic – curriculum and pedagogy - which is central both to national educational traditions and to international orthodoxies of reform.

REMAKING CURRICULUM AND PEDAGOGY: CONTEXT AND RATIONALE

The growth of the knowledge economy, writes the EC, "demands fundamental rethinking of traditional conceptions of knowledge, its 'transmission,' 'delivery' by teachers and acquisition by students. It raises questions about the assessment and learning of knowledge and the more demanding resources of skills, attitudes and motivations to learn. It questions curriculum content and the prioritisation and compartmentalisation of 'subjects.'"[16]

This vision of comprehensive transformation is very different from that of the traditionalist conservatism that has often been a force on the European right. The legacies of authoritarianism and colonial nationalism are not extinct. In the late nineties, the Aznar government attempted to impose a "Spanish" history curriculum on the dissident nationalities of Catalonia and the Basque Country; likewise, in 2005, the French parliament decided that school history courses "should recognise in particular the positive role of the French presence overseas, notably in North Africa."[17] However, these are occasional regressive episodes rather than signs of a rising trend. Much more prevalent is a curriculum that overturns the established frameworks of curriculum, pedagogy and assessment in the name of quality and innovation, and that presents itself not as conservative but as a force for modernisation.

This modernisation is not without appeal. Later in the article, we sketch some of the ways in which it attaches itself to what used to be thought of as the progressive critique of educational traditionalism. But it is nonetheless thoroughly neo-liberal, in its conceptions of educational financing, of the relation between education and equality, and of the purposes of curricular and pedagogic change. Its pledge to overturn established frameworks of curriculum, pedagogy and assessment in the name of quality and innovation needs therefore to be called into question at several levels.

First of all, it is clear that there is no intention of replicating the levels of funding that sustained earlier waves of modernisation. Writing of higher education, Viviane Reding, then European Commissioner for Education and Culture, explained as much in 2003: the "economic situation does not permit further significant public money to be invested …"[18] This was not least because the returns from investment in education were disappointing. The performance of education was stagnating, the French ministry of education told teachers' unions in 2004, even though student numbers were falling and investment in human resources had increased.[19] Similarly, the Deutsche Bank concluded that "an appreciable improvement in the quality of educational outcomes is not necessarily linked to an increase in educational expenditure."[20] In consequence, the rule of more from less should apply. Education must look for efficiency savings, and private investment must increase.

Nor are educational resources equally available to all. Modernisation is presented as desirable and practicable for entire populations, but this universalism is in practice heavily qualified by differentiation and inequality, reflecting the effects of the knowledge economy itself. Phillip

Brown points out that the American and British economies, for instance, "are characterised by enclaves of 'knowledge work' along large swathes of low-waged, low-skilled jobs."[21] This fundamental disparity structures educational provision. On the one hand, at higher levels, competition becomes more intense: there are "too many contestants chasing too few prized jobs,"[22] and the acquisition of the credentials that underpin individual success in the labour market becomes for the middle class an absolute and often desperate priority. On the other hand, there is the problem of those who are in practice "excluded from the knowledge society because they do not have at their disposal the means to participate in it."[23] The gap between these two social categories has grown remorselessly and is a defining feature of the new system.[24] Despite its inclusive rhetoric of change, the new kind of modernisation is thus profoundly dichotomised, in ways that earlier policy documents anticipated. In 1996, a Commission White Paper (the "Reiffers Report") had castigated the reforms of an earlier period for their attempts to introduce egalitarianism to societies which could never be other than stratified; it endorsed the "filtering mechanisms that are founded in a form of individual competition" and accordingly insisted on a double prioritisation – of the education of élites, and of the most disadvantaged and socially difficult.[25]

In the curricular designs of national states, this divided approach has been replicated – albeit that the resources devoted to the élite are somewhat greater than those enjoyed by the less successful groups.[26] Governments presided for many years over arrangements in which a pattern of apparently common schooling of 5/6-16 year-olds masked intricate arrangements through which social differentiation was translated into educational distinction. But such arrangements did not work perfectly. One of the problems was the process of "academic drift" which occurred within common systems that lacked the capacity to establish strong forms of distinction between different groups of students; it was not with unalloyed pleasure that policy-makers observed the increasing number of students taking the bac général in France in the early nineties, nor the rapid rise in the student population of Italian universities.[27] At the same time, there were plainly problems with the disengagement of the least successful students from the entire certification process; while élite groups, unhappy with qualifications systems that had become massified, demanded forms of certification that identified the highest-performing students. (In England, this latter demand led to the creation of an A* grade in 16+ exams, distinguished from a mere 'A' grade, and marking out the *crème de la crème*.)

In response to such difficulties, governments are attempting to establish mechanisms to differentiate between students at an earlier point in their school careers, claiming that in this way they will re-engage with the most disaffected, meet the needs of middle sectors seeking relatively high levels of competence, and satisfy also the demands of more powerful groups. It is on this basis that we should understand a number of national policy shifts. Inscribed in the Spanish LOGSE legislation of 1990 was the principle of dignifying "vocational education" and directing towards it a large part of the less successful population of state school students, while the majority of pupils in the private sector were turned towards the *bachillerato*[28]. In England, the Blair government insisted that schools should abandon mixed ability teaching, no matter what the research evidence in its favour, and brought forward the age at which students could be placed on a vocational track[29]. In Italy, the Moratti reforms involve a labyrinth of post-14 options, including the establishment of "vocational schools" through which education and work-based training will be linked – a measure that the main union federation, the CGIL, thinks will "increase social differences in our country."[30] The French "Thélot Commission," set up by the Raffarin government to redesign the basic principles of schooling, outlined a rationale for this type of change: "the idea of success for all must not be misunderstood. It does not at all mean that the school must ensure that all its pupils achieve the highest possible level of qualification. That would be an illusory goal for individuals, as well as an absurdity in social terms, since educational qualifications would no longer be linked, even vaguely, to employment structures."[31] (Building on Thélot, the present French minister of education, Gilles De Robien, has used the November 2005 riots to bring to an end a policy of massification whose heralded goal was to bring 80 % of an age cohort to baccalauréat level. Youngsters of fourteen years old would be allowed to enter apprenticeships and the mission of the collège unique, to provide all-round education until the age of 16, would thus be terminated.)

In Germany, where the "orienting" of pupils to different types of secondary education occurs at the end of the primary years, there is growing pressure to move the key moment of selection to a later point.[32] This Europe-wide pattern of convergence, in which 14/15 has become the age at which educational destinies are settled, suggests that while there is a strong trend towards mass participation in certificated education, this movement is qualified by processes of rationing and curricular segregation.

"BASIC SKILLS" AND "QUALITY"

The definitive settling of educational destinies at 14/15 is accompanied by a new emphasis in 5-14 education on the acquisition of "basic skills" and of "quality" in the delivery of them. This says much about the acceleration of governments towards a policy orthodoxy, in which "all" students – save those substantial numbers schooled in the private sector, and those state school students identified as "gifted and talented" or as possessing "special needs" – will experience a common and narrowly-defined core, whose effectiveness will be measured by international comparisons.[33] Berlusconi, ever reducing neo-liberalism to the level of absurdity, defined this vision in the starkest terms. The new purposes of Italian education are understood under the heading of the 3 'I's' – impresa (business), informatica, inglese. But it is in England that the project is most detailed and advanced: primary schooling is dominated by "National Strategies" for Literacy and Numeracy which – according to Blair's advisors – should occupy more than 50% of the school timetable.[34] These detailed and prescriptive strategies are claimed by the Blair government as its greatest educational success, responsible for increasing the success rate of 11 year olds in national tests; a "National Literacy Framework" extends the approach to the first three years of secondary schooling. The English example is emulated elsewhere, though without as yet reproducing the directedness in small things which is the distinctive feature of anglo-schooling. In France, Thélot recommends a common basis ("socle") of essential skills, that will be the basis of personal success and social integration: "reading, writing, competence in spoken language, familiarity with mathematical operations, the ability to use a computer, (knowledge of) English as a tool for international communications, knowing how to live together as members of the same society."[35]

Moratti's intention of bringing to an end the tempo pieno of Italian primary education will have a similar effect in defining the essentials of schooling: the reduced hours of learning will squeeze out subjects such as music from the common curriculum, leaving them to be taken as options. Likewise in Germany, the disappearance in the 1980s of the *Rahmenrichtlinien* of an earlier period has led to a narrowing of the curriculum, in which reading, writing and arithmetic occupy a central place. Everywhere, it is intended that these long years of basic skills acquisition will be subject to strong regulation in the form of national systems for the testing of students, with learning processes evaluated on the basis of reference points external to the school, and with systemic effectiveness measured by international comparisons of student achievement. The performance of English children is measured at 5, 7. 11 and 14; in Germany, all sixteen states have introduced *Vergleichs* – or *Parallelarbeiten* – systems, where schools set end of year tests that are marked on the basis of common criteria; even in Hesse, often recognised as the homeland of progressivism, numerical marks have replaced teacher evaluations in the end-of-year assessment of young children. By these means, what is de facto a centralised curriculum is developing, while arching above and influencing national frameworks of evaluation is the international PISA system of performance indicators. PISA, developed by the OECD, is especially important in this respect. By establishing a common, transnational set of criteria for student performance, it lends authority to proponents of neo-liberal reform: when, in 2002, the sample of German students fared poorly in the PISA tests, this gave enormous impetus to reformers.

The ability of schools to inculcate basic skills, and to demonstrate rising levels of attainment, is seen as central by governments, and contributes in important ways to the legitimisation of government policies. But policy design is also based on other principles, more generous in their attention to individual need. It claims to be developing forms of education that enable individuals, each at their own level, to respond to the challenges of a risk society in which successful employment depends upon constant adaptation to new labour market situations. A spokesperson for the French employers' federation, MEDEF, identifies the issue in these terms:

> The essential recommendation that I would offer is to make the individual responsible for their own courses of study … There is no longer a role for education in setting normative frameworks; the role of the collectivity is to make possible the maintaining of individual competences … Thus the logic of précarisation is no longer connected with fear or insecurity; although an individual may experience a period of non-employment, so long as he remains 'competent' he can redirect himself towards another job.[36]

"PERSONALIZED" LEARNING

The relationship between the highly normative emphasis on basic skills and the insistence that the education of the future must be based upon the individualised acquisition of competences is not without its tensions, especially at the point where competences are defined in terms of the qualities of initiative, creativity and team-working supposedly required by post-fordist economies. The tensions are managed through a number of strategies, in which the requirements of the neo-liberal social order are translated into the language of personal development. Among such strategies is responsibilisation – what Gewirtz calls "the process of inculcating a culture of self-discipline or self-surveillance among welfare subjects," through techniques that include portfolio assessment, homework policies and home-school agreements.[37] The responsibilisation of individuals requires the personalisation of the curriculum, a process in which traditional subject boundaries – so Thélot and others expect – will dissolve.

Personalisation – *Individualisierung von Lernprozessen, personnalisation des parcours* – has nothing in common, British ministers insist, with the child-centredness of an earlier era. Whereas the ideal of progressive education was a notion of individual development and self-realisation combined to greater or lesser extent with an idea of collective emancipation, personalisation operates with more explicit norms; it is an attempt to identify the individual learning strategies that are most effective in reaching an externally given and predefined outcome. It does not involve a curriculum claiming to respond primarily to students' interests, nor a pedagogy that encourages children to "be themselves." On the contrary, it is based on offering support to individual students in order that they may reach defined targets. The support includes the use of ICT [computers] and of "learning mentors," not necessarily qualified teachers, to work with students in small groups. Above all, it means "curriculum choice," particularly during the 14-19 stage, when academic and vocational pathways become available.[38] At this point it becomes difficult to distinguish personalised learning from a form of selection, and the appeal to individual need folds into the reproduction of social divisions. This involution is particularly clear in Thélot's presentation. For his committee, children will realise their different potentials according to their preferences, their talents and their efforts, and to assist in this process, the school will organise itself along three different pathways, defined by the outcomes towards which they are headed.

OPPOSITION

Announcing a programme of modernisation is one thing, implementing it quite another; governments here face a number of obstacles – each more structural than contingent – that arise from the limited capacities of states and the continuing strengths of opposition as well as the contradictions between what states intend and what market-influenced systems let them do. "As if anything could be restructured in Italy," wrote Leonardo Sciascia. The jibe, directed originally against the demand of those who kidnapped Aldo Moro for a "restructuring of Italian prisons" applies just as much to the Berlusconi/Moratti reforms.[39] Berlusconi may have made the 3 'I's the cornerstones of a rhetoric of modernisation, but several embedded factors in practice work against him. Humanist cultures are still dominant in secondary education; primary teachers are still conscious of past achievements; the "softening up" of teachers under Thatcherism, which prepared the way for New Labour's pedagogic régime, has not been replicated. In any case, the long history of underinvestment in Italian education leaves it ill equipped to deliver credible universal programmes of English and ICT, while business involvement is more likely to fragment the provision of vocational education than to improve it.[40]

The position of other states is little better. In the mid-nineties, many commentators were sceptical about the Spanish project of "profound curricular reform" at a time of "severe budgetary restrictions;" such problems continue to undermine the public system, have resulted in the growth of sharp regional inequalities, and fuelled the expansion of the private sector.[41] In France, discussion of curricular reform takes place amid controversy over long-term of cuts in teacher numbers, and is still shaped by traditions at odds with the precepts of new modernisation. The strikes of lycéen(e)s in 2005 were motivated in part by opposition to proposals for local validation of the baccalauréat that students thought would create new, regionally-based hierarchies of status. More generally, the large-scale teachers' strikes of 2003 were driven not just by issues of pension rights and changes to contractual status but by a sense that an entire social project – "the school of the republic," egalitarian in vision if not in actuality – was under threat. Thus, for Samy Johsua, the strikers saw themselves as guarding "the frontier between one system of values and another;"[42] and for Bertrand Geay the strike-generated *assemblées générales* of schoolworkers and citizens were lived as "retour à l'essentiel." In defiance of neo-liberalism, and the sense of disintegrating habitus, which accompanied it, the founding principles of public education were reactivated, and knowledge and the conditions of its diffusion became matters for public appropriation.[43](Geay 2003:12)

England appears to be something of an exception in this context. Unlike France or Italy, Blair's government can claim it "owns" the curriculum and pedagogy of schools; the battles against professional influence and political radicalism have been won; New Labour has created a strong educational state, that works to highly specified targets, is closely managed, and – compared to the 1990s – well-financed. If the neoliberal claim to be installing a "quality" system of mass education, is anywhere being realised, then it must be in England. But, in fact, the problems of the English classroom remain considerable, and judged in terms of Labour's wish to create a "world-class" education system, its reform has been far from successful. This English impasse reveals much about the meanings of "quality," as it is deployed in neo-liberal discourse. The Blair government regards the National Strategies for Literacy and Numeracy as its most strikingly successful achievements, and thinks them responsible for a rise in the level of 11 year olds' performance in national tests between 1998 and 2003 (a rise which has since levelled off). Academic researchers tend to argue the contrary, concluding that "there is little evidence that (the NNS) has been an 'undisputed success,'" and that in the case of both strategies "traditional patterns of teaching have not been dramatically transformed." On the contrary, "far from encouraging and extending pupil contributions to promote higher levels of interaction and cognitive engagement, most of the [teachers'] questions were of a low cognitive level designed to funnel pupils' responses towards a required answer."[44] These specific, classroom-focused criticisms are amplified by wider studies: large-scale projects of standards-focused reform, employing a uniform pedagogy and curriculum content across schools of widely different class and ethnic composition, have not resulted in continuous improvement over a medium-term period, even where that improvement is measured in terms of standardised tests; they have not reduced socially-based inequalities of achievement and have in some cases increased them. At the same time, they have narrowed curricula and induced stress among students and teachers.[45] The capacity of systems like the English to bring about enduring qualitative change is thus questionable on several grounds.

THE STRUGGLE FOR QUALITY AND PURPOSE

These problems lead to the equivocal heart of neo-liberalism's programme of modernisation, and link the English experience to that of other countries more closely than first appears. Marketed as what its exponents like to call a "step-change" in educational quality, it, in fact, proposes a dismantling of the curricula and pedagogies which sustained the uneven advances of the post-war decades, in favour of a model whose most notable features are sharp social segregation, strong managerial direction and an emaciation of teaching and learning. Quite contrary to neo-liberalism's self-presentation, the model is widely perceived by both traditional humanism and progressivism as the contemporary face of educational regression. Humanism objects to its emphasis on "the basics" and its preference for defining educational outcomes in terms of marketable skills rather than disciplinary knowledge. Progressivism is appalled both at its curricular impoverishment and at its profoundly undialogic model of learning, in which negotiation with the experiences and capacities of learners find little place. There is, of course, implicit in these judgments a certain unjustifiable nostalgia – traditional humanism left most students confined within a curriculum framework even narrower than that currently proposed; and in the period of the grands moments pédagogiques of progressivism the initiatives of teachers, students and parents could not cancel out an overall pattern of inertia and inequality. But this should not reduce the force of their critiques. They express a sense of degeneration that is at present one of the main resources that neo-liberalism's opponents possess. Among sections of teachers in England and Spain, there is deep dissent from the principles of neo-liberal pedagogy and curricula. In Germany, both reform pedagogy and traditional conceptions of Bildung offer potential vantage points for criticism. For French opponents of the Raffarin and de Villepin governments, their reforms amount to a trivialisation of the republican project, in which curricula will be attenuated and the inculcation of values of citizenship reduced to the management of behaviour. For Italian protestors, the Moratti reforms threaten to "impoverish culture and learning" and replace well-founded knowledge traditions with a new and under-funded competence-based curriculum.[46] The difficulty, as always, is to translate these growing critical perceptions to a persuasive and popular alternative.

NOTES

[1] For a classic statement of this dual responsibilty, see Tony Blair, "The Power of the Message" *New Statesman 29* September 1995, p.15

[2] The chapter draws from work in progress undertaken by Ken Jones (with Richard Hatcher, Nico Hirtt, Samy Johsua Jürgen Klausenitzer, Rosalind Innes, and the Colectivo Balthasar Gracian) on the impact of neo-liberal change on European education; and on Nathalie Duceux's writing on educational conflict in France, particularly 'Éducation : Du rapport Thélot à la loi Fillon' in *Critique Communiste* No. 174, Winter 2004 pp. 12-22

[3] Laval, C. and Weber, L. (co-ordinators) (2002) Le nouvel ordre éducatif mondial Paris, Syllepse

[4] European Commission *Growth, Competitiveness, Employment* Luxemburg 1994; *Teaching and Learning, towards the knowledge society*, Luxemburg 1995.

[5] Presidency Conclusions, Lisbon European Council (2000), available at http://ue.eu.int/ueDocs/cms_Data/docs/pressData/en/ec/00100-r1.en0.htm (accessed January 2006)

[6] ibid

[7] ibid

[8] European Commission *The Concrete Future Objectives of Education Systems*. Brussels, European Commission 2001

[9] See the discussions in Nico Hirtt *Education et formation 2010: comment Mme Reding a fait accelérer la cadence* www.ecoledemocratique.org 7 March 2005; Laval and Weber op.cit. pp. 123-126.

[10] European Commission *European Report on Quality of School Education: sixteen quality indicators* Brussels, May 2000

[11] European Commission, White Paper *European Governance* 2001 http://europa.eu.int/comm/governance/governance_eu/nat_policies_en.htm, accessed January 2006.

[12] See Nafsika Alexiadou (2005) 'Europeanisation and Education Policy' in D. Coulby, C. Jones and E. Zambeta *World Yearbook of Education 2005: globalisation and nationalism in education* London, Kogan Page.

[13] Op.cit p. 137

[14] Roger Dale (2004), 'Forms Of Governance, Governmentality And The EU's Open Method Of Coordination in Larner, Wendy and Walters, William (eds) (2004) *Global Governmentalit: new perspectives on international rule.* London: Routledge. 174-194

[15] Christian Laval (2005) Traité Constitutionnel et Éducation: le trompe d'oeil européen www.écoledémocratique.org, accessed January 2006

[16] European Commission, European *Report on Quality of School Education: Sixteen Quality Indicators European Commission*, Brussels 2000.

[17] The Guardian 16th December 2005 ('The Empire Strikes Back' by Jon Henley)

[18] *Libération* February 12, 2003.

[19] Quoted in Duceux, (2004) p.13

[20] Deutsche Bank-Research, *Mehr Wachstum für Deutschland* 2003, p.7

[21] P. Brown (2003) 'The Opportunity Trap: education and employment in a global economy' *European Educational Research Journal* 2.1 2003 pp.141-179, p.150.

[22] Brown, *op.cit*. p.152

[23] Commission of European Commission (1996) (*Accomplishing Europe through Education and Training: report of study group on education and training*) quoted in Nico Hirtt, Im Schatten der Unternehmerlobby. Die

Bildungspolitik der Europaischen Kommission. In *Wiedersprüche* 83 pp. 37-51

[24] 'From 1986 to 1999, the 10% of students experiencing the least schooling saw investment in their education increase from between 2,850 and 16,5000 francs. The 10% receiving the most schooling received extra investment in the range of 254,000 to 438, 000 francs.' Pierre Merle *La Démocratisation de l'Enseignment Paris: La Découverte* 2002, p.91

[25] Commission of European Commission (1996) *Accomplishing Europe through Education and Training: report of study group on education and training Brussels*, European Commission, p. 71

[26] In the case of France, Pierre Merle calculates that the gap between the resources available to the least and the most 'scholarised' students actually increased between 1988 and 1998. *La démocratisation de l'enseignement Paris:* La Découverte 2002, pp. 86-91. There are even stronger disparities, of course, in relation to family 'investment'. In relation to Spain, the Colectivo Baltasar Gracian concludes that 'if the difference between the sectors of higher and lower incomes in terms of average total family spending is 1 to 3, in the area of spending on education it is 1 to 44'. (See Grupo de estudios del colectivo Baltasar Gracián 'Fracaso Escolar: *La estructura del fracaso escolar en la ESO dentro de la Comunidad de Madrid.* II' in Crisis, Número 4, Noviembre 2003.

[27] For figures, see Roberto Moscati (1998) 'The Changing Policy of Education in Italy' *Journal of Modern Italian Studies* 3.1 pp. 55-73

[28] 'The Ministry of Education has published recently … that in the year 2002/3 they had already succeeded in getting 42% of those who continued post-compulsory education into the vocational cycles, whereas in 1995/6 there were only 35%.' *Crisis*, Numero 3 2003

[29] See Stephen Ball *The More Things Change … Educational research, social class and 'interlocking' inequalities* Institute of Education, University of London 2003. DfEE Schools Building on Success London: The Stationery Office 2001.

[30] European Industrial Relations Laboratory (2005) 'The government approved two implementing decrees on the reform of the education and training system' http://www.eiro.eurofound.eu.int/2005/04/inbrief/it0504102n.html, accessed January 2006

[31] Thélot, quoted in Nathalie Duceux 'Du rapport Thélot à la loi Fillon' *Critique Communiste* 174 Hiver 2004, pp. 12-22.

[32] See for instance the frequent comments of Andreas Schleicher, Head of the OECD's Education Indicators and Analysis Division. E.g. William Pratt 'Schools face new criticism' *Frankfurter Allgemeine Zeitung 17th September 2004, English edition.*

[33] For the extra provision made in England for 'gifted and talented' students, see the DfES website. www.standards.dfes.gov.uk/giftedandtalented. For the significance of the international comparisons of achievement made possible by the OECD's PISA project, see Laval and Weber op.cit and OECD *School Factors Related to Quality and Equity – Results from PISA 2000* Paris, OECD 2005.

[34] The civil servant Michael Barber, quoted in Robin Alexander 'Excellence, Enjoyment and Personalised Learning: a true foundation for choice' in *Education Review* 18 (1) Autumn 2004 15-33, p.19

[35] Commission du Débat National sur l'avenir de l'école (rapport provisoire, aôut 2004) (The Thélot Report)

[36] Quoted in Samy.Johsua, L' idéologisation libérale du rapport entre « compétences » et « savoirs », paper to Congrès Marx International III Paris 2001

[37] Sharon Gewirtz, *The Managerial School* London: Routledge 2002, p.161

[38] See the Education Minister David Miliband – 'Choice and Voice in Personalised Learning' speech to the DfES/Demos/OECD conference on *Personalising Education: the future of public sector reform.* London, May 2004 pp. 3-4

[39] Sciascia *The Moro Affair & The Mystery of Majorana* Manchester: Carcanet Press 1987, p.18

[40] Legambiente – Scuola e Formazione: Scuola Pubblica: liquidazione … di fine stagione, cifre, dati, commenti sui tagli operati dal Governo ai danni scuola pubblica February 2004. accessed on the website http://www.lascuolasiamonoi.org/articolo.php?id_art=152, January 2006

[41] Javier Doz Orrit 'Problems of Implementing Educational Reform' in Barrett Brown and O'Malley 9eds) *Education Reform in Democratic Spain* London, Routledge 1995. For post 2002 developments see the journal Crisis http://www.colectivobgracian.com/

[42] Johsua, S. (2003) 'Un mouvement plus antilibéral que'altermonialiste' *Le Monde de l'Education* No 317 September p.15

[43] Geay, B. (2003) 'Un processus de réattachement à l'institution' *Le Monde de l'Education* No. 317 September p.12

[44] M. Brown et al 'The Role of Research in the National Numeracy Strategy' British Educational Research Journal 29 (5), 2003 and F. Smith et al 'Interactive whole-class teaching in the National Numeracy and Literacy Strategies' Strategy' *British Educational Research Journa*l 30 (3), 2004.

[45] Andy Hargreaves *Teaching in the Knowledge Society* Open University Press Buckingham 2003.

[46] See the call of the 'Stop Moratti' campaign, national conference, Florence 2004, available on the website www.lascuolasiamonoi.org

The Centrale des Syndicats du Québec And the Struggle Against Neo-Liberal Schooling

VÉRONIQUE BROUILLETTE

Understanding history makes it possible to anticipate the future.

Quebec's education history is a very special history in the context of North America. Emerging out of a more collective French culture that has had to fight hard to survive – in creating an economic and political base and in preserving its language and its history – Quebec schools have had to develop some very distinct characteristics. On the surface, these characteristics can be seen, for example, in a secondary system that ends in the 11th year, followed by the transition to CEGEP, a post-secondary educational institution leading either to university entrance after a two-year program of general studies or to the technical trades after a three-year program. It's a structure that offers all Québec children a better chance than most at a decent education, however much it may still fail far too many of them. If we go deeper, the collective nature of Québec's schooling (as well as the impact of modern capitalism on it) is perhaps best seen in the development of the Québec Teachers Union (now the CSQ).

Québec has, relatively speaking, a high level of unionization (41.2% in 2003, compared with the Canadian average of 32.4% and under 15% in the United States). This union movement has provided a major impetus for social change in the province's recent history. Since the Quiet Revolution of the 1960s, the province's unions have been pivotal in the building of public services, as we know them today. The Québec Teachers Union has played a major role within this movement.

Shortly after the Quiet Revolution and the establishment of a genuine public educational system, the Centrale de l'enseignement du Québec (CEQ[1]) published a manifesto whose title evokes the spirit and the ideology of the era: *Our schools serve the ruling class*.[2] At about the same time, the other two major union confederations published their own manifestos: *Ne comptons que sur nos propres moyens (CSN) and L'État, rouage de notre exploitation* (FTQ).[3] The year was 1972, when the three major union confederations formed their first common front to conduct public sector negotiations. It proved to be a decisive moment in the history of the Quebec union movement. It was a time of radicalization in the Québec union movement, the glory days of radical unionism for those who lived through this era. The three confederation presidents were eventually sentenced to one year of imprisonment after recommending that striking members not concede to the injunctions of the government that had just passed special legislation to force strikers back to work.

The CEQ manifesto has remained an enduring document because of its powerful criticism of capitalist society. It argued that schools helped reproduce social inequalities and the dominant ideology. It asserted that the "common enemy" of the workers was capitalism and that teachers, in solidarity with the working class, had their own battle to fight against this system. And it laid out the following conditions that would be essential to take on the "common enemy" in the schools:

> … an understanding of the mechanisms of exploitation in capitalist society; the pursuit of the analysis of the role of schools in transmitting the dominant ideology and in the reproducing of social classes; the collaboration of teachers with students and other workers in order to define a new type of school adapted to the real needs of workers; the collaboration of teachers with all workers to clearly define a project for a classless society which an increasing number of workers would support; a solid organization at the grassroots level, in the workplaces, in order to lead the battles required to attain the final objective.[4]

More than thirty years later times have changed. The Québec union movement no longer uses Marxist class analysis and terminology in its publications. It does, however, continue to defend the same values it did thirty years ago: among others, social justice, fairness, equal opportunity and solidarity. These values have been undermined since the beginning of the 1980s when the New Right emerged as a major force within the educational system. In its wake, the progressive role of the state and unions in society have come under increasingly critical attack, the private sector has been powerfully championed against public services, and governments and school boards have increasingly moved to support this policy direction.

To give some sense of what this direction has meant for Québec, I want to re-apply the rationale of *Our schools serve the ruling class*, adapting it to the current context. Although the socio-political context in Québec has changed a great deal over the past thirty years, several aspects of the analysis continue to be relevant today. It is still undeniable that our "schools are not neutral," that "our society is based on the profit motive" and that our "schools transmit the dominant ideology," as the CEQ affirmed in 1972.

THE GROWTH OF THE NEW RIGHT IN QUÉBEC EDUCATION[5]

Our schools serve the ruling class borrowed from theories on reproduction[6] according to which schools are the mirror image of capitalist society and reproduce social and economic inequalities. Children from privileged backgrounds, it argued, had bourgeois cultural capital, of the kind schools transmitted. They did better than children from disadvantaged backgrounds because these children didn't have this kind of cultural capital. This school of thought marked a key moment in the sociology of education, but its determinist dimension has often been criticized. It certainly neglected the ongoing resistance of students and teachers and parents to make a more caring and effective school system. But one thing is certain: its emphasis on the ideological aspects of education are as relevant today as they were when the CEQ manifesto was written, perhaps more so. Education is clearly not "neutral." There is an ever-widening gap between the neo-liberal view of education and an opposing democratic viewpoint.

What distinguishes the present from the 1970s is that educational reform not only has to meet province-wide objectives (emerging out of contending social forces within Québec), but it is also strongly influenced by the concepts – and the power – of the major international economic organizations. These include not only the OECD (for education as a whole) and the WTO (for higher education), but even the World Bank, which is mostly focussed on the developing world. The educational model we have to follow, according to all these organizations, is one focussed on "the production of human capital in the context of a knowledge economy." This utilitarian model is the one political and economic authorities have been explaining to us since the 1980s. Schooling, we are told, has to be seen as an instrument to increase productivity and therefore the competitiveness of the nation. In the context of a "knowledge" economy or society – whether it's service sector employment or the development of information and communications technologies – education has become a strategic issue for state systems.

Beyond the intervention of international organizations, the New Right assault on Québec education has been led intellectually by an international combination of neo-conservative and neo-liberal ideologues – inspired in politics by people like Margaret Thatcher and Ronald Reagan and in the economic world by theorists like Milton Friedman and Friedrich Von Hayek. Québec has had its full share of those advocating minimal state intervention, recourse to private services in public affairs, and the elevation of the so-called natural laws of the marketplace to the status of social regulation. In the 1980s we took in, along with everyone else, the arguments coming from Great Britain, the United States, Australia and New Zealand to dive headlong into reforms stressing educational choice, privatization, competitiveness, outcomes-based education, and standardized testing. Increasingly, it became difficult to defend our schools in terms of their emancipatory role in educating enlightened citizens. The capitalist model became more and more dominant.

In Québec, neo-liberalism's most ardent defender is the Montréal Economic Institute, a right-wing think tank whose Canadian counterpart is the Fraser Institute. The Montréal Economic Institute believes that the free market is the most effective method of distributing goods and services because it responds quickly to clients and optimizes freedom of choice Its conceptual framework is limited to cost/benefit analyses, which, in the view of the Institute's analysts, is the most rational and objective method of understanding the world in which we live. In education, it took up the attack launched on "public education's monopoly" – an attack devised at the end of the 1980s by Jean-Luc Migué and Richard Marceau, two of the founders of the Montreal Institute.

The extent of the power of market ideology in the school system is perhaps best seen in the extensive emphasis now placed on "entrepreneurship."[7] It has now become a core education "competency" to be valued by students and staff; it is even set out as one of the broad areas of learning in the curriculum. The current Charest government has announced its plans to develop entrepreneurship-study projects at the elementary and secondary school levels. As is the case in other curriculum areas, the government will be relying on the cooperation of major employer associations. No similar plans involve the union movement.

We have also begun to see an extraordinary new thrust of privatization, for which the "Ubisoft affair" has served as a leading example. In the winter of 2005, Québec's Ministry of Education[8] granted a subsidy of $5.3 million to create three certificates of college studies for programs developed by a regional CEGEP but dispensed in the offices of Ubisoft, a multinational video game firm, located in Montréal. The Université de Sherbrooke, the Université de Montréal and the Université du Québec network also signed cooperation agreements with this firm in order to develop graduate programs and partnership agreements. Ubisoft now has the right to supervise training and research topics over a wide range of programs.

SCALING BACK SERVICES, CENTRALIZING CONTROL

The continued undermining of the social role of the state has led to significant budget cuts and to the devolving of authority to individual institutions.

The scope of the Québec government's involvement in education has been scaled back, as attested by the lowered percentage of gross domestic product (GDP) invested in education since the 1990s. In 1992-93 Québec spent 8.7% of its GDP on education. By 2002-2003 that figure had moved down to 7.5%. For the 2002-2003 education budget of $8.5 billion this reduction represents a loss of $2.55 billion.[9]

Québec's education system has experienced both decentralization and centralization as have other education systems in Western countries.

In many ways the decentralization (for all its rhetoric of local democracy) has been developed in the service of increased centralization. It has been largely engineered to make the implementation of central decisions more effective, particularly in reinforcing ministry control of educational "outcomes" and their assessment. It also opens the schools to increased commercialization, with more emphasis on the consumption of "educational services" from private sources.

The move to centralize via decentralization involved the establishment of governing boards for local schools as well as increased autonomy for the post-secondary CEGEPs. It was part of what Patricia Broadfoot[10] calls the transition to the Evaluative State. It is a transition that has also seen very significant resistance, especially among the province's schoolteachers. Québec's teachers were mobilized on this issue and forced the government to restrict its activity to reviewing the role and the composition of governing boards. Furthermore, the legislative framework that was adopted ensured a balance between union representation and parental representation, and respected the professional autonomy of school staff. At this point in the struggle, the results represented significant gains for the education community. Some years later, the government tried to amend the legislation to require school governing boards to adopt success plans, including high-stakes practices through graduation rates and accountability. Ministry plans required that all schools adopt measures to ensure their graduation rates would increase by two percentage points per year, not only an impossible task but a wrong-headed one. Once again, however, union mobilization forced the government to withdraw its proposals and the plan for high-stakes practices in the province's elementary and secondary schools was scrapped. This was a significant union victory in Québec.

For postsecondary education, the struggle against the imposition of high-stakes practices proved more difficult.

The CEGEPs are now bound by these practices, which means they are required to set targets for improving graduation rates in their success plans, which are included in their strategic plans. The college success plans must take into account the quantitative targets established by the ministry of education. The CEGEPs are the only educational institutions in Québec that must submit their institutional strategies and policies to an external evaluation agency – the College Education Evaluation

Commission.[11] This agency was founded in 1993 – along with the new emphasis on targets – when the CEGEPs were granted the official status of higher education institutions and acquired more autonomy. Alongside this program centralization (via decentralization) came major program cuts, as has been the case with most of the New Right reforms of this era. At the same time as the CEGEPs were decentralized, the Government of Québec, in pursuit of its "zero-deficit" budget, cut $260 million in college subsidies – more than a quarter of their funding between 1994 and 1998.

In 1999, the universities were hit head on by the high stakes practices when "performance contracts" were instituted between universities and the government. Universities were asked to establish performance indicators oriented towards the rationalization of the programs offered, the level of efficiency of management and specific projects in order to link universities financial resources to strategic priorities.

Overall, the New Public Management, which has inspired successive education ministers since the 1990s, has been a disaster for Québec education. Focussed on the management of productivity in education – which amounts to the policing of a standardized curriculum by test scores – those in charge of Québec education have neglected the development of real content in our classrooms. Or, to put it another way: human capital production is increasingly driving out genuine learning.

CONSUMER CHOICE

The market is everywhere in our lives. *Our schools serve the ruling class* made that point in 1972, and it is just as true today, even more so. Neo-liberalism is an increasingly dominant ideology, influencing nearly all spheres of society including the public services, which are borrowing methods from private business, in order to become more "productive, efficient and effective." A "virtual market" model has developed in education. It's called a virtual market because it is difficult to reduce education to the status of a classic free market. "Education benefits not only individuals, but also families and society as a whole. The service supplier may choose the consumer, the roll-out is monitored, clients are sometimes required to consume (school attendance is compulsory) and there is not an award system supply and demand."[12] Neo-liberals don't like this reality, but they press on regardless.

Neo-liberal ideology has infiltrated education in Québec in a subtle and gradual way. One of the most striking examples is the use of the term "school clientele" to designate students, a term that has become ubiquitous among educational stakeholders. With the use of this term, education is increasingly perceived as a private rather than a public asset. Based on this principle, parents should have the freedom to choose the best education for their children, be it private or public. Being "free to choose" – to cite the title of a book by Milton Friedman – is prescribed as one of the best ways of improving the quality of education and to give the most disadvantaged students access to the best schools.

In Québec, the focus on choosing schools led to the annual publication of a report card on schools in a major magazine with broad circulation, *L'actualité*. This report card, compiled by the Montreal Economic Institute and the Fraser Institute, claims to help parents choose schools for their children based on the performance of the institutions – reflected in their test scores. However, this report card says nothing about the real "performance" of the schools; it merely tells us where the good (high-scoring) students go: to schools that select their students on entrance, usually the private schools. Parents, who want the best for their children – a very normal parental impulse – are therefore tempted to choose private schools, which appear, at first sight, to show the best results. The social selection in this picture is, of course, neglected, but it's there in the back of most ambitious parents' minds as a plus for the private system.

Opting for private schools is on the increase in Québec, and it is having an impact on public education. Between 1997 and 2003, the number of elementary and secondary school students registered in the private network has increased by nearly 9,000, while the public network lost over 35,000 students. The drop in the number of students in the public network is also attributable to population decline. The contrast is even sharper with the secondary schools, where 17.6% of francophone students are enrolled in the private network. This proportion is even higher in urban areas (over 20%) and in the Montréal area (30%).

Across Canada, Québec has the highest percentage of its students enrolled in the private school network. This situation is mainly attributable to the scope of the public funding provided to private education. While a number of Canadian provinces do not fund private education, the Québec government provides 43% of the income of private schools. As a percentage of funding per student in the private system, the Québec government covers 60% of what it pays for a student in the public network. In 2004–2005, the Québec government spent $375 million on private schools. Since private schools are mostly the preserve of affluent students, this funding arrangement only exacerbates the inequalities between public and private schools. Public funding of private schools, according to some analysts, should be seen as a form of school vouchers.

Québec has toyed with implementing the concept of school vouchers several times. It mostly took the form of certificates redeemable for a specified sum that parents might use for their children's education. These vouchers could be submitted to the school of one's choice, either public or private. A working group set up by the Bourassa government recommended the implementation of vouchers in 1986, but the recommendation was not adopted. The concept resurfaced in the Québec election campaign of 2003. The election platform of Action démocratique du Québec, a right-wing party led by Mario Dumont, proposed the implementation of school vouchers that would "introduce a market mechanism" into education, which would encourage "schools to compete" in order to meet the demands of parents. Stimulated by competition, schools would be compelled to provide the best service in order to attract and retain students, the ADQ argued, and the best schools would expand to the detriment of "ordinary" schools.

Education stakeholders, including Quebec's federation of school boards and federation of private schools[13] strongly opposed this proposal. In a research report produced for the CSQ based on the experience of other countries, Antoine Baby[14] argued that it is false to claim that school vouchers have made it possible to improve learning or increase parents' satisfaction. He showed that, in many cases, school voucher programs have caused greater social segregation and gaps in success levels between different communities; that resources allocated to the administration of the program are usually deducted from monies allocated to public education; that nearly everywhere, the private network has expanded to the detriment of the public network and that education personnel have often been penalized by fluctuations in client groups. The impact of this research report, combined with the strong opposition to vouchers from a broad spectrum of education stakeholders, doomed the proposal. At least for a while.

The growth of a consumer rationale for education can also be seen in the development of vocational, technical and continuing education. In these areas, the "consumers" are the bosses, who will be hiring the "products" produced by their local schools. Here the Ministry of Education still plays a prominent role, even though the boundaries between private and public education in this field are often blurred. In Québec, both professional and vocational education was designed as a centralized system mainly under the jurisdiction of the Ministry of Education. Over the last few decades, the ministry has been severely criticized – particularly by the business sector – for not giving adequate consideration to the needs of the job market. Since the early 1980s, the result has been a number of education reforms focussed on aligning the system more closely to the needs of job-market stakeholders. The introduction of a competency-based approach and the establishment of services for businesses in school boards and CEGEPs are two examples of this alignment. Although the ministry of education remains the major "supplier" of vocational and technical training programs, the role of Emploi-Québec,[15] the ministry responsible for employment, has increased in scope in this sector, particularly since federal government funds for labour force training have been repatriated.

In the wake of centralizing decentralization, the school boards and the CEGEPs have taken on many new services for business and have acquired the right to create their own diplomas for adults – certificates for both vocational studies and college studies. Services for business are self-financing and represent a lucrative sector for educational institutions. Since they were deregulated in the 1990s, there has been a proliferation of short-term training programs and of sometimes fierce competition between public educational institutions in the recruitment of students. A range of "made-to-measure" training, more or less based on the "just in time" management principle, seems to be the preferred path. As for continuing education, the educational institutions have borrowed many practices from businesses to the extent that the development of services for businesses may be perceived as diverting the educational mission of schools to that of a marketing mission.

TRANSMITTING THE DOMINANT IDEOLOGY: COMPETITION AS THE ENGINE OF DEVELOPMENT

Our schools serve the ruling class showed how schools transmitted capitalist ideology, reproduced social inequalities (women, the disadvantaged and ethnic minorities) and repressed any attempt to alter social relations by imposing discipline, maintaining a social class hierarchy and promoting individualism. Another, perhaps more updated way of putting this, says that education mirrors the dominant ideology: that the values advocated by this ideology (individualism, performance, effectiveness, efficiency, etc.) are all reproduced in the education system, which contributes to maintain and even exacerbate social inequalities.

Not everything is black and white, of course, and Québec's education system is neither entirely neo-liberal nor entirely social democratic; it is a combination of the two. Neo-liberalism, however, has become the dominant ideology today, reflecting a much more aggressive form of the social regulation that is now part and parcel of globalization. In education, as is the case for all public services, this worldview borrows from not only an economic doctrine (neo-liberalism) but also from a management model (the New Public Management).

Several aspects of the education reforms undertaken in Québec for the past fifteen years take up a number of the key New Right ideas. The cult of performance is expressed in the institution of "success" plans in school boards and CEGEPs and "performance" contracts in universities. Validation of the private sector is reflected in the public funding of private education. A consumer rationale is expressed in the annual publication of a report card on secondary schools and in the development of made-to-measure training programs.

These ideas, applied to the world of education, help reproduce inequalities by instituting a winners-and-losers logic. Faced with the increased enrolment of Québec students in private schools, the public schools began to adopt the practices of private schools, creating special, selective programs requiring special application. Various programs, such as sports-studies, arts and sciences, international education and all the rest, have been developed in elementary and secondary schools to attract "good" students. As in the private schools, many programs select the best students on entrance – a way of showing that public schools are of the same quality as private schools. These selective programs have had the effect of creating a three-tiered education system: private schools, selective programs in public schools for the "good" students and regular classes for "ordinary" students. The publication of the secondary schools report card has contributed to reinforcing these divisions. In this context, regular classes end up taking in a much higher concentration of students with difficulties (especially those who don't do well on standardized tests), even though the research clearly shows that a classroom mix is beneficial for students in difficulty and does not harm good students.

Neo-liberalism applied to education represents a real threat to public education, and it is up to citizens to demand that public education be protected. The struggle to counter "group-think" is not being fought in vain. It has been productive on a number of occasions, and it is important to highlight the sources of resistance. The concept of school vouchers was not adopted in Québec. Elementary and secondary schools were spared the practice of high-stakes tests. The law also prohibits any form of commercial advertising in Québec schools, and only Sweden has similar legislation.

A "FINAL OBJECTIVE" FOR 2006?

Here, the analogy between *Our schools serve the ruling class* and an updated analysis of education is not as obvious. In the 1972, "the final objective" referred to the Marxist ideal of a society of equals without social classes. The Left of the 1970s proposed radical change to the social order. In today's context, it is the Right that is proposing a change to the social order, whereas the Left has been reduced to resisting the Right's agenda. The "final objective" of the Left remains a "social agenda" whose definition is still in progress.

The union movement and Québec's Left in general continue, nevertheless, to demand a more fair and equal world. In this they join thousands of people around the world in an ongoing struggle to achieve a more humanized form of globalization, to defend public services, the environment, women's rights, etc. The CSQ is part of this struggle, particularly though the Brundtland Green Schools (BGE) movement that it initiated some ten years ago. A BGE is a school that "acts locally while thinking globally" in order to promote a sustainable future. It is a place where people take tangible, ongoing action in order to help create an ecological, peaceful and democratic world in solidarity with all working people.

The 1972 manifesto called for "defining a new type of school." The CSQ has followed through with this recommendation. It did so in 1980 with its "School Proposal"[16] and in 1995–1996 by launching the Estates General on Education, a public reflection on the education system that addressed all of society. On that occasion, the CSQ published a new manifesto, entitled: "A different school system for a different society,[17]" including a *Declaration of Principles* adopted at the CSQ Congress. The mobilization associated with the Estates General made some advances, particularly in extending the secularization of the school system and in improving early childhood services. But it did not succeed in slowing the development of a neo-liberal view of education.

Today, taking the offensive is more necessary than ever before. The principles of democratic education and the action needed to achieve it have to be brought front and centre. And the broadest possible solidarity has to be built for this struggle – across the union movement, the wide network of community groups, and all the organizations that bring people together within the school system. This is the challenge the CSQ faces in the coming years.

NOTES

[1] The Centrale de l'enseignement du Québec (CEQ) changed its name to the Centrale des syndicats du Québec (CSQ) at its general congress of 2000 in order to reflect members working in sectors other than education.

[2] Confédération des syndicats nationaux (CSN). *Ne comptons que sur nos propres moyens.* The English translation, *It's Up To Us*, can be found in Daniel Drache, ed., *Quebec: Only The Beginning* (Toronto: New Press, 1972).

[3] Fédération des travailleurs et travailleuses du Québec. L'État rouage de notre exploitation. The English translation, *The State: Exploiter of the Working Class*, can be found in Daniel Drache, ed., *Quebec: Only The Beginning* (Toronto: New Press, 1972).

[4] Centrale de l'enseignement du Québec. *Our schools serve the ruling class*, Dossier adopted at the CEQ Congress of June 1972. All excerpts cited have been adapted, as the original English translation is currently unavailable.

[5] For a more in-depth view of the development of neoliberalism in education

in Québec in the context of globalization, see Jocelyn Berthelot (2006). Une école pour le monde. *L'éducation québécoise dans un contexte de mondialisation* [Schools for people, schools for the world. Quebec education in the context of globalization], French publication forthcoming in September 2006.

[6] See in particular Bourdieu and Passeron, *Les héritiers* (1964) and *La Reproduction* (1970) and the key work by Beaudelot and Establet published in the early 1970s, *L'école capitaliste en France*. In the United States, Bowles and Gintis published a similar analysis in 1976 in *Schooling in Capitalist America.*

[7] Entrepreneurship in the French curriculum (*Programme de formation de l'école québécoise*). In the English curriculum (*Québec Education Program*), it is called *Personal and Career Planning*.

[8] The Ministère de l'Éducation, du Loisir et du Sport du Québec, referred to here as the Ministry of Education.

[9] Secretariat intersyndical sur les services publics (interunion public service coalition) (2005). *Access to quality public services: our priority!* Québec, joint publication of the Syndicat de la Fonction publique du Québec, du Syndicat des professionnels du Gouvernement du Québec and the Centrale des syndicats du Québec, p. 12. http://www.sisp.qc.net/sites/1677/documents/services/CSQ_colloque.pdf

[10] Broadfoot, P. (2000). « Un nouveau mode de régulation dans un système décentralisé : l'État évaluateur. » *Revue française de pédagogie*, no 130. Janvier-février-mars 2000, pp. 43-55.

[11] The Commission d'évaluation de l'enseignement collégial.

[12] Berthelot, J., op cit.

[13] The Fédération des commissions scolaires and the Fédération des établissements d'enseignement privés.

[14] Antoine Baby (2003). *Des bons ? À quoi bon ? Une analyse de la question des bons d'études* [Vouchers, what for? An analysis of the school vouchers issue]. Note de recherche no 50, Québec, Centrale des syndicats du Québec (unavailable in English translation). See also CSQ, *School Choices and Vouchers*, D11278A, April 2003.

[15] Ministère de l'Emploi et de la Solidarité sociale.

[16] *Proposition d'école.*

[17] *Une école différente pour une société différente.*

The New Right Agenda and Teacher Resistance in Canadian Education

LARRY KUEHN

Enough is enough. This was the message sent by British Columbia teachers when they embarked on a two week strike in October 2005 that had been declared illegal. The trigger for the walkout was the British Columbia legislature imposing yet another contract on teachers, extending, in fact, a contract imposed three years earlier. Behind the teacher response, however, was a much broader and deeper set of issues, which are in no way limited to British Columbia. Over a number of years now the province's teachers have experienced an increasingly restrictive environment in how they do their work and the resources they have available to do it. In many ways, the strike was a reaction to teachers feeling unable to offer their students the education they knew was possible.

The B.C. teachers' reaction has become a common teacher reaction around the world. As a result, while this strike was specific to British Columbia, it hit a chord with many teachers across Canada and internationally. When the courts imposed a ban on the B.C. Teachers' Federation paying strike pay to its members, other Canadian teachers contributed more than $1 million to a hardship fund for B.C. teachers. The union representing the college faculty in B.C. immediately set up a $200,000 fund to buy $50 grocery vouchers for teachers and support staff on the picket lines. Teacher unions in the U.S., Latin America and Southern Africa sent messages of support. Teacher unionists in Mexico and Honduras held demonstrations at the Canadian embassies, calling on the government to abide by the labour rights accorded in the International Labour Organization (ILO) conventions.

This wide support for the demands of British Columbia's teachers reflects just how broadly government policies in the era of neo-liberal globalization have undermined public education and its promise of equity and democratic participation. B.C. teachers wanted improved conditions for teaching – limits to class sizes and provision of more resources to meet the incredibly varied needs of students with special needs and the large number of students for whom English is second language. They sought a reasonable salary increase, rather than the three years of zero that the government was imposing. And they wanted respect for professional and labour rights, with the right to full collective bargaining restored.

These are hardly radical demands. All of them, in fact, only asked for a return to the situation that had existed only a few years ago, but had been taken away by the current right-wing government. These are demands of teachers that would be similar in any country, whether rich or poor, where the promise of public education has been undermined by the economic and social policies that have been sweeping the globe in the last two decades.

In the case of British Columbia, the provincial government used legislation to strip from the teacher contract class size limits and supports for students with special needs. This allowed for the elimination of more than 2,600 teaching jobs between 2002 and 2004, about 8% of the teaching force. In the past, B.C. teachers had traded salary increases to leave money for the better teaching conditions that were then eliminated by legislation. As a result, salaries had fallen behind – and then they lost teaching conditions they had, in essence, paid for.

The union representing teachers, the B.C. Teachers' Federation (BCTF), actively opposed these policies. The government identified the union as the prime opponent of its policies and moved to isolate and weaken the BCTF.

The government refused to consult the union on its education plans and policies, while, at the same time, it consulted extensively with parent and administrator associations and provided them with significant funding (and direction) to lend their weight in support of government policies.

Earlier, the government legislated a takeover of the College of Teachers, the teacher certification board. It had been made up of 15 members elected by the educator members of the College and five appointed by government. A slate of teacher candidates, chosen through consultation among BCTF union locals, consistently filled the elected positions. The new legislation fired all the elected College board members and appointed government supporters to the College board. The government's aim was to use the College to control teacher practices. It didn't reckon, however, on the strength of the union, and eventually the government was forced to back down and return the majority of the board positions to elected teachers. The BCTF organized a teacher boycott of the College fees required to maintain a teaching certificate. Some 20,000 teachers sent their College fees to the union to be held in trust, rather than to the College. If the government had not backed down, it would have had 20,000 teachers without valid teaching certificates.

This successful challenge to government policy and legislation helped to develop confidence that collective action, strategically directed, could force government to change policies that were unilaterally adopted and seen as unfair.

Despite this confidence, an illegal strike presented real risks. A union that challenges a government in this way is fortunate to come out of the situation without serious harm. The courts did fine the BCTF $500,000, which went to charities, and would have increased the fine substantially if the teachers had not voted (by 77%) to end the strike when they did. A mediator made recommendations that gave both sides a basis to close off the conflict. Although there was no direct salary increase, teachers regained some of their losses by an insurance fee rebate and $40 million was applied to harmonize salary grids around the province – together these were worth 4%. The money not paid to teachers during the strike all stayed in the school system, with $20 million specifically to address large classes and class composition problems – the main demands of teachers. Another $56 million was given to districts and schools to purchase books and other resource materials – the first real infusion of money for this purpose in a decade.

The key message from this was one of strength in solidarity. The government could not smash the union – because it was not allowed to, whatever it might have wanted. Teachers were together. All the school support staff joined the teacher picket lines. Two areas of the province were shut down for a day each when other unions withdrew services. Students held rallies in support of teachers. Parents brought goodies to the picket line – so many that people complained about gaining weight in this action. Student teachers joined in and felt a part of the collective. Geoff Bickerton in *Canadian Dimension* concluded that the strike "helped strengthen the teachers' union and the entire labour movement as they prepare for future battles with the government."

THE NEW RIGHT IN EDUCATION

Two weeks after the end of the B.C. teacher strike, Michael Apple, in a seminar with the BCTF, described four elements that make up the alliance of the right in its current manifestations in the U.S.: neo-liberalism, neo-conservatism, authoritarianism and the new managerialism. All can be seen at work in Canada in general, and particularly in British Columbia. All have areas of overlap, but also distinctive elements. When they operate together, despite some differences among them, they form a very powerful right-wing force.

Neo-liberalism

The neo-liberal program is largely about making the market supreme, reducing the size of government and promoting individualism over social decisions. It operates through reducing government revenue through cuts to taxes, particularly for the well off, and then using lower revenue as an excuse for cutting services. The market, rather than collective social decisions and rights, is seen as the appropriate way to make decisions, particularly about allocations of resources and, consequently, services. Privatizing is the preferred way of providing consumer choice in markets. Where direct privatization is not possible, the aim is to simulate markets through some process to provide individual choice, such as vouchers and charter schools.

Privatizing takes several forms. The most explicit is providing public funding for private schools, as is done in B.C. and some other provinces. In B.C., private schools receive from government 50% of the per pupil amount provided to public schools. Most of the private institutions are religious schools, including Catholic, evangelical Protestant, Sikh, Muslim, along with several secular, elite schools. Even Fundamentalist Mormons (a breakaway from mainstream Mormonism) who practice polygamy and have teenagers marry men several decades older, get public funding to run their own private schools. The percentage of students in private schools has grown to 10%, climbing every year since government funding was made available to private schools.

Other forms of privatization are rife throughout the public system. Probably the most common is fundraising. When the central government cuts back on resources, it is the parents, teachers and local communities that are turned to in order to fund what would otherwise be missing. This, of course, produces further inequities as an individual school's ability to raise funds is largely a function of the socio-economic status of the school community. In Vancouver alone, some elementary schools raise hundreds of thousands of dollars, while others can only manage a few thousand.

Teachers end up funding the schools as well. If teaching resources are not available through a school budget, many teachers will spend their own funds to make the teaching situation tolerable. A Canadian Teachers' Federation study indicates that the average amount a teacher spends in a year on their classroom and personal professional development is $1000. One school district in B.C. (Surrey), proudly reported to the press that teachers in the district had contributed $25,000 a year to pay for lunches for hungry students to make up for the funding for the program that had been cut by the provincial government.

The government has also been floating suggestions that it might amalgamate school districts into large units that would take over administrative functions – and open the way for privatization of services such as school buses, payroll and maintenance. A provincial agency has already been created to promote and facilitate P3s – public, private partnerships – to build hospitals, bridges and schools.

Privatization and private-like government services advances the neoliberal program of making the individual-as-consumer sovereign. The rights of public employees are seen as getting in the way of "flexibility." This means that those who work in providing a service should have no guarantees of consistency in their employment. Unions and collective agreements, of course, get in the way of this flexibility, so they are prime targets – and opponents – of neo-liberal policies.

One major effect of reducing the size of government is a reduction in its redistributive functions. Eliminating or reducing services offered on a somewhat equal basis to everyone has little negative impact on those at the top of the income levels, but a lot of negative impact on those at the bottom, and often on those in the middle as well. The rich can always afford alternatives, whether education, health care or swimming pools.

While neo-liberalism is about reducing the size of government, it is not about reducing the impact of government. The role of the state is seen as creating laws and conditions that assist market forces allocate goods, services, capital and labour. "Deregulation" is a key part of this process.

Neo-liberals often describe regulations as "red tape," with negative connotations. While some regulations in any area may be unnecessary, many of them have been adopted as protection of the public interest and the protection of individuals against the predations or simple neglect of the public interest by corporations. In the case of B.C., one element of the electoral platform of the neo-liberal B.C. Liberal government was to eliminate "inflexible" regulations. A few examples indicate what this really means. Many environmental regulations about logging were replaced with a "results-based" system that has made the forest industry largely self-regulating in deciding whether it is meeting environmental standards. Car dealers were given authority to set up a system for regulating themselves. Child labour is now allowed as early as 12-years, with only a parent signature approving it, rather than a government agency having to determine that it is safe and appropriate.

Deregulation was applied to education, as well. The private, for profit, post-secondary training institutions (of which there are more than 1,000 in B.C., the most in Canada) were told to self-regulate, rather than being accredited through a government process. Services for students with special needs in the school system were also deregulated by doing away with targeting of funding for high-incidence special needs and English as a Second Language support. Much of the funding to support students with special needs was rolled into one block from the province to the school boards. Previously, it had been targeted, so at least that specified amount went to specifically meet the needs of students with special needs. Similarly, targeted funding had existed for ESL students and for textbooks, but was all rolled into block funding.

Provisions for limits to class sizes and staffing ratios for teacher-librarians and special education teachers were stripped from the teacher collective agreement by legislation – which we noted above – another form of deregulation. The rationale for all of this was to provide flexibility and to create an education system that had more "choice," the code word for individualizing and privatizing what had been understood as rights to particular services. At the same time that this flexibility was created, the government adopted financing policies that reduced the capacity of school districts to deliver services. Reducing the fiscal capacity of government – one element of the neo-liberal program – while giving flexibility to school boards meant that the responsibility to manage the reduction in services was now downloaded to the boards. The rationale for reducing the real funding to school districts was a provincial budget deficit – one that had been created by giving huge tax reductions to the highest income individuals and to corporations.

While "flexibility" and "choice" have become watchwords, this does not mean that real control has been handed off to the local or school level. As is common with neo-liberal policies, central control reaching into the classroom was intensified, using the mechanisms and techniques of the new managerialism. More about this link later.

The neo-liberal approach is certainly not unique to British Columbia. The World Bank and the International Monetary Fund rigorously impose neo-liberal policies on the national school systems of the countries that are dependent on their loans. The World Bank, in fact, has a whole program in its education branch aimed at providing ideas and examples to support the privatization encouraged by its lending policies. The Bank also identifies teacher unions as a major impediment to the implementation of these privatization and marketization policies.

To one degree or another, neo-liberal policies have been repeated across Canada. In fact, as the new millennium arrived, total spending on public education in Canada declined for the first time. Ontario went through nearly a decade of a Conservative government that pioneered similar policies to those adopted by the B.C. Liberals and is now experiencing the rationalization and intensification of these policies under its new Liberal government.

Neo-liberal/Neo-conservative

The terms neo-liberal and neo-conservative are often used interchangeably, particularly in Canada. Michael Apple makes a useful distinction between them. He sees neo-liberalism as focusing on the market and the role of the state in maintaining and promoting the market. Neo-conservatism, on the other hand, is more focused on social issues. Neo-conservatives see a strong role of the state in enforcing issues of "morality" and intervening to impose their understanding of "morality" on everyone. They oppose many of the social changes that have been taking place, such as the right to choice on abortion and the current hot button, same-sex marriage.

In the U.S., the Republican Party is effectively an alliance between these two groups, which, when united, are a very powerful force. Several states, for example, had referendums on same-sex marriage on the ballot in 2004, which may well have been a factor in George Bush winning a number of these states. Commentators have suggested that when a larger than expected group of voters showed up to vote against same-sex marriage, they stayed to vote for Bush – and his neo-liberalism – while they were there.

In Canada, to a considerable degree, the attitudes on social and cultural issues are also what distinguish the two major federal parties, though there is not a clear demarcation line between the two. The federal Conservative party tends to have somewhat of a balance between neo-conservatives and neo-liberals (though likely more of the latter). The federal Liberal party, on the other hand, is largely neo-liberal, but still has something of a neo-conservative wing. The provincial B.C. Liberal party has become a coalition of these two tendencies and includes members of both the federal Conservative and Liberal parties.

To a lesser degree than in the United States, neo-conservative political views spill over into the politics of education. One Canadian school district, however, stands out in contrast to most others – Surrey, B.C. In the 1970s, the Surrey school board prohibited the use of a slide-tape show that showed historical examples of racism in the province, including the exclusion of people from India, anti-Chinese riots early in the 1900s and the internment of Japanese-Canadians in the 1940s. The school board said that talking about racism would promote racism, and that it was better to leave the topic untouched. More recently, the district spent more than $1 million on legal expenses in an attempt to keep three children's books about families with same-sex parents out of the classroom; they took their case all the way to the Supreme Court of Canada, before losing it. Since then the Surrey district has banned a student play about the murder of a gay young man that took place in Idaho – a play put on in many other school districts in the U.S. and Canada.

Neo-conservative ideas are also demonstrated in a demand by some parents for "traditional" schools. These have been created as schools of choice in several districts in the B.C. Lower Mainland. These schools generally require students to wear uniforms and are expected to have more teacher-centred pedagogical practices and strict discipline. These appeal to a conservative ideal of what schools were like in the past, real or imagined, and a desire for more control over children. As it has turned out, the curriculum tends to be the same in these schools as in all other public schools; these days nearly all schools are pretty traditional. The most noticeable difference from other public schools is the students in uniforms.

Authoritarianism and the new managerialism

Apple suggests that Canada seems to have less of the authoritarian tendencies that are visible in the U.S., perhaps because it is less militarized. The new managerialism, however, is flourishing in Canada. It is an ideology and technology of control through management systems and is exemplified by the testing and comparison system in the *No Child Left Behind* approach being taken in the U.S. It is an accountability system based on techniques borrowed from the accounting system in business. In its extreme form, the new managerialism claims that what can't be measured, can't be managed, and thus everything that is important should be measured. It is an approach being adopted in government, in general, not just in education.

Some have described the approach as "steering from a distance" and Janice Gross Stein in the Massey Lectures described this system as defining the role of government as "steering, not rowing." In other words, government maintains control by setting the objective and then having a feedback system of data that lets it know whether its direction is being followed or some new directive needs to go out to adjust the direction. As is obvious, this fits very well with neo-liberal ideology and politics. It shifts the role of the state from delivering service to setting the conditions for service, whether the service is delivered by government or by private, for profit or non-profit organizations. In theory, it distributes decision-making in the system to the local level. However, this is an illusion, because the most important decisions, those about what we want to accomplish, are made centrally, mostly by technocrats – largely committed to capitalist organization – rather than by democratically elected officials. What is decentralized is responsibility, but not authority; the responsibility is the responsibility to meet the central objectives, not to satisfy the particular community to whom the service is being delivered. Obsessive alignment with central goals turns the new managerialism into a soft form of authoritarianism.

While these approaches are in place to one degree or another everywhere in Canada, the approach in British Columbia is clearly one of the most extreme. In B.C., every ministry must develop a "service plan" that sets out the objectives of the ministry and how they are to be carried out and evaluated. The ministry of education plan places its focus on "achievement." The focus is not on the broader category of "learning," that might have many elements that cannot be measured, but rather specifically on achievement that can be measured. It is telling that the service plan is lacking two elements that most would consider integral to education – teachers and curriculum. This is because in an input-process-output model, they have said that only outputs are important and they must all be measurable. Inputs – teachers, class sizes, socio-economic status of students, disabilities, etc. – are not important. Only outputs in the form of test results or other data are important. Processes – curriculum, pedagogy and democratic participation – are subordinated to the measurable output – or simply ignored.

New technologies play an important role in providing the information necessary to enforce alignment and compliance. A central, web-based database is being implemented to hold information about every student in the province over their entire school career. Each teacher will have a computer in their classroom to enter data – attendance, marks, comments, personal information about students. While privacy is supposed to be protected, having all the data in a database will allow for extensive central monitoring, right down to the classroom level.

A recent book by a World Bank economist, Tim Harford, points out the absurdity of this everything-important-can-be-measured position when he says "Economics is about who gets what and why.... There is much more to life than what gets measured in accounts. Even economists know that." Unfortunately, not all education bureaucrats or politicians seem to know that.

Even though teachers are not in the B.C. ministry service plan, its centralized approach reaches into the classroom and attempts to steer what's done there through a many layered control system. The top level is a school district accountability contract. This is a document that each school board must agree to with the ministry of education. It sets out the achievement objectives for the district including targets for improving the data on achievement. Elements that must be in the contract are defined by the ministry.

Each school must have a School Planning Council made up of three parents elected by parents, the principal and one teacher selected by the teachers. Teachers and others who work for any school district are prohibited from being elected as a parent representative on these councils, even if they have children in the school. The School Planning Council is to develop a school growth plan that must be consistent with the provisions of the district accountability contract with the ministry. The school staff is then obligated to develop ways to ensure that what happens in their classroom is consistent with the school growth plan which is consistent with the district accountability contract which is consistent with the ministry service plan. The objectives and measures at all these levels must have numbers, so the primary ones being used are the Foundation Skills Assessments, standardized tests of literacy, writing and math at Grades 4 and 7, and provincial subject area examinations at the Grade 10 and 12 levels.

All of this feeds into the individual "choice" ideology of neo-liberalism. The right-wing think tank, the Fraser Institute, takes the information from the provincial tests to develop provincial school rankings, from top to bottom. The Global-CanWest owned newspapers publish these rankings annually, taking up many pages in their papers. While it started in B.C., the Fraser Institute and CanWest partnership has now taken this ranking system to most provinces in Canada.

The Fraser Institute rankings produce distorting effects. One district official in a high result and high socio-economic status district has claimed district results are a result of "better genes" in his community. Teachers and students in schools at the bottom of the list feel that all the success in growth and learning that has taken place in their schools is devalued. All of this is done in the name of providing market-like information to improve choice – even though few people have the capacity to choose to move to a high-ranked school.

The Liberal government in Ontario has also adopted an intense target and testing approach, largely following the advice of former Ontario Institute for Studies in Education (OISE) Dean, Michael Fullan. Before becoming the key education advisor to Ontario Liberal premier, Dalton McGuinty, Fullan played a central role as a consultant to Tony Blair's New Labour government, helping it develop a set of neo-liberal policies that far exceeded Margaret Thatcher's reforms. Fullan's former colleague and writing collaborator, Andy Hargreaves, has now challenged Ontario's decision to follow Blair's direction, pointing out in a *Toronto Star* article, that "the most recent research demonstrates that the so-called British achievement gains, based on imposed short-term targets and aligned testing, are mainly an illusion – partly because the tests just got easier each year."

GLOBAL POLICY BORROWING AND POLICY IMPOSITION

How does it happen that these neo-liberal/neo-conservative and new managerial policies and practices are showing up everywhere, albeit with some local variations? Globalization is clearly part of the answer.

The economic objectives of schooling have become dominant because of the belief that "human capital" is a key factor in economic success against global competitors. Education has always been seen as having some economic objectives, but not as dominant everywhere as they are now.

Part of the process that has produced this new "common sense" about the way that education can be improved from a human capital perspective is what has been called "policy borrowing." It is basically a number of processes that produce a consensus among decision-makers that a particular approach is appropriate.

Policy borrowing is what happens among the countries at the top of the development scale. Those countries at the bottom adopt these policies through policy imposition. The IMF and the World Bank, as a condition of loans for education, require that specific policies be adopted, and they happen to be the neo-liberal policies that they impose.

The roots of the currently dominant approaches in education go back to the Reagan administration in the U.S. and the A Nation at Risk report. This report argued that economic problems in the U.S. were a result of an education system that had fallen behind other countries. However, the aim of the Reagan administration went beyond reshaping U.S. education; it was concerned to develop an international agenda.

In the early 1980s, the United Nations agency, UNESCO, had been promised funding from the World Bank to develop a set of international indicators. It would presumably have incorporated a wide range of educational purposes, including its social and cultural aspects since social and cultural elements are part of its mandate. The Reagan administration was not at all happy with the policy directions of UNESCO since the majority of its members were pushing policies opposed to U.S. hegemony. The Reagan administration pulled the U.S. out of UNESCO and got the education indicators funding moved to the Organization for Economic Cooperation and development (OECD). The indicators that the OECD developed, along with the testing system for outcome measures, the PISA tests, have a narrower focus, consistent with the OECD's specific economic mandate. Education is viewed primarily as an economic factor and one of the prime producers of human capital. The OECD has been a primary link in the policy borrowing process and in promoting the new managerialism in education. The annual publications of the OECD indicators and the PISA results are used extensively to make comparisons between countries.

RESIST AND RECLAIM

Two directions seem necessary as responses to the dominant position that has been achieved by the Right in its various forms – neo-liberal, neo-conservative and new managerialist. One is resistance to these directions. The other is to reclaim the public, social and democratic space that public education should be about.

The 2005 BCTF strike is certainly one example of that resistance. Similarly the Ontario teacher two-week political protest strike in the mid-1990s was a powerful statement of opposition. The regional general shutdowns by public and private sector unions in areas of Ontario over several months were also a loud message of resistance to the reshaping the Conservative government of that time was doing to the public sector. Many quieter forms of resistance are staged on a day-to-day basis, whether in opposition to excesses in standardized testing or to increasing authoritarian governance of the schools.

Resistance is not necessarily successful in making immediate changes – in fact, it often does not. It still plays an essential role. It disrupts the message of the dominant views. It reminds the public and ourselves that there are other ways of looking at the world, that these are issues that should be open to continuing democratic debate, not compliantly accepted.

Resistance is not enough. Challenging the dominance of the right in education requires not just being defensive, but rather recapturing the promise of public education. Universality and equity can never be achieved in a private system, yet universality and equity are the underlying requirements for an education system that supports a democratic society and prepares citizens for universal participation. To get back to the principles and ideals of public education, it is important to redefine and reinforce the purposes of public education in the current context and projected future. What should a public education system for the 21st Century look like?

One approach taken by the BC Teachers' Federation was a process it initiated and financed to engage the public and teachers in answering this question about the future of public education. The BCTF created a commission of five panelists to travel around the province and listen to views of what public education could be. Only one of the five was a teacher union activist. The others included the parent of a student with special needs, a church minister, an Aboriginal leader and a retired school superintendent.

As they met with different groups, they asked them not to talk about all the problems in the system as it exists, but rather to think about their ideals for what public education could be. To stimulate their thinking, people were asked to consider their positive image of an educated person, and then decide what qualities an education system needed to achieve that ideal. After hearing from hundreds of people, the group synthesized the views they heard into a statement of ideals and principles – the *Charter for Public Education.*

To spread these ideals and principles and to be an ongoing presence in the discussions of education, the group initiated a Charter for Public Education Network. It is open for anyone interested in education to join. Its purpose is to keep the ideals of public education before the public and to continually remind people of the ongoing investment that a society must make if it is to maintain a public system that serves everyone and is the basis for a democratic society.

This is but one of many possible approaches to stimulating public discussion of the question "What kind of public education do we need for a democratic society in the 21st Century?" Whatever approach we take, reclaiming the ideals of public education and translating them into an improved public education system calls for us to engage our communities. It is only in collectively redefining what we want public education to be that we can have an effective challenge to the program of the Right.

The New Right Triumphant: The Privatization Agenda and Public Education in Australia

RAEWYN CONNELL

During the last twenty years in Australia, a well-developed public education system has been severely damaged by neo-liberal attacks at both state (provincial) and national levels. The new policy regime, introduced in a context of panic about globalization, has reversed previous patterns of growth, damaged popular confidence in education, and intimidated teachers and administrators. Though there are some signs of a revival of commitment to public education (Esson, Johnston and Vinson 2002), Australia is certainly at an extreme among developed countries, in terms of the impact of the neo-liberal market agenda on public institutions. It may serve as a cautionary example for educators in other countries; but also, perhaps, as a source of ideas for responding to global neo-liberalism.

THE POLITICAL CRISIS OF PUBLIC EDUCATION

Constitutionally, Australia is a federation on the US/Canadian model. Education is a responsibility of the states; but since World War II, financial power lies with the federal government, which has used this power to intervene in all policy areas. Until the advent of neo-liberalism in the 1980s, federal governments of both major parties, Labor (a social-democratic union-based party) and Liberal (meaning conservative, the party of urban capital, in coalition with rural conservatives) had used this power to build up public education, following a "nation-building" agenda (Pusey 1991).

By the 1960s Australian governments had built a mass school and advanced education system, strongly centralized, controlled by bureaucratic techniques, in principle universally available, in practice fairly cheap and remarkably uniform across the country. It had produced near-universal literacy, and was widely credited with being a force in the country's then rapid economic growth. A wholly public university and college system was expanding fast. An impoverished Catholic school system, surviving from ethnic-religious conflicts of the nineteenth century, increasingly modelled itself on the state schools.

From the 1960s to the early 1980s a wave of democratic experiments occurred in this system. There were attempts to decentralize bureaucracies, and shift control over curricula to schools and teachers. There were strong attempts to widen access to education, to make the system friendlier to girls, to families in poverty, and to children from Aboriginal and recent immigrant backgrounds (Rizvi and Kemmis 1987). There were innovations in curriculum, such as an expansion of social science teaching. There were experiments in pedagogy, such as student-directed courses in universities, and a growing number of experimental participatory institutions such as learning networks, high school "annexes" and co-operative pre-schools.

By the late 1990s these developments, with few exceptions, were halted, in retreat, or vanished. Market agendas were triumphant (Marginson 1997a). The democratic critique of education bureaucracies had been twisted into an argument for market solutions. The Catholic system had been successfully aligned with elite Protestant schools rather than state schools. State education institutions were being privatized from within, with massive re-structuring and disruption in TAFE (technical and further education) and higher education. People had begun to talk about state education becoming a residual system, serving only those who cannot compete in the market.

The speed and strength of this change has shocked many people, and to a degree has paralysed opposition from the public sector. Privatization in education has not flowed from a public policy debate that the privatizers won. In fact there has been little educational argument for privatization at all. The agenda has been imported ready-made into education from the international strategy of social reconstruction through the market.

In the late 1970s and 1980s, Western politics was captured by a reformed conservatism (widely known as neo-liberalism, in Australia "economic rationalism"). This movement of ideas and policies rejected both the class compromises of the post-war decades and the welfare state institutions which were built on those compromises. In their place, private enterprise was to be unleashed as an engine of prosperity and allowed to operate untrammelled in all spheres of life – including education.

As in other areas of public policy, neo-liberal policies in education were not introduced as a result of public demand. They were introduced by coups. Neo-liberals gained control of relevant governments or portfolios and then re-structured education on new lines. Some moments were dramatic. The Greiner state government in New South Wales, for instance, gaining power after a long-serving and popular Labor premier had retired, restructured public education to force schools to compete with each other, and dramatically increased the number of "selective" high schools catering to middle-class parents. The Kennett state government in Victoria, led by a cowboy-style politician of short-lived popularity, similarly tried to reconstruct the public school system as a market of competing firms.

It is important that Labor governments, too, became part of the neo-liberal drive. The college and university system was re-structured by surprise under the Hawke Labor government from 1987 on. The federal minister of education, Dawkins, introduced fees, started a scramble of amalgamations and competition, and stimulated the growth of an entrepreneurial management elite that now effectively controls the universities. Currently the state Labor government in Western Australia is restructuring its public school system on an "outcomes-based education" model, a typical neo-liberal scheme to induce competition and "accountability."

Another Labor initiative has been a national rationalization of technical education, introducing an "Australian Qualifications Framework." This has tended to modularize technical education and the old apprenticeship system is now quite dead. There has been a recent tendency to expand vocational education courses in high schools, a reform mainly addressed to non-academic working-class students. This is popular with parents, and with some of the pupils, though it has caused inter-sector problems and delivers little in the way of portable qualifications.

Perhaps the most important trend, however, has been gradual: the growth over the last thirty years of a massive system of public subsidies for private schools. As a result of ethnic conflicts in colonial times, Australia had a large, though poor, system of Catholic parish schools staffed mainly by nuns and brothers. When this system reached terminal crisis in the 1960s, nation-building governments began to subsidise it, and in the 1970s public money became the main support of church schools. Under neo-liberalism, this has turned into a huge subsidisation of private schools in general, building them up as a market-based alternative to the state school systems.

The neo-conservative media (Australia has a media oligopoly dominated by two right-wing moguls, Murdoch and Packer) have assisted, by mounting steady attacks on public schools, public school teachers, and public sector teacher unions. An ideology of parental "choice" has been vigorously promoted, with the corollary that parents who care about their kids will always choose private schools. As a result of this ideological offensive, plus the lowering of relative costs by heavy subsidies to private schools, a significant shift of enrolments into the private sector has been occurring. This in turn is gleefully reported in the media as proof of the greater desirability and success of private schooling.

PRIVATIZATION IN EDUCATION: A CLOSER LOOK AT THE PROCESS

The underlying process in privatization is the transformation of some good or service into a commodity, which is circulated through a market and given value by market transactions. The process requires the constitution of a commodity; the creation of market institutions; and the creation of needs that the market will supply.

The commodity. What is the commodity being marketed by private schools and privatized colleges and universities? To say it is "education" or "learning" or "instruction" is true but unspecific. Marketing something that is already available (more or less) free is futile, like trying to market air. Therefore extreme privatisers want to shut down the free source. Short of this solution, what private schools crucially market is their difference. Specifically, they market their capacity – real or imaginary – to provide students and their families with an advantage in academic competition, social connection, labour market position or security. School systems all over the world are enmeshed with systems of social inequality (for a fine contemporary study from Ireland, see Lynch and Lodge 2002), and this gives the concern with educational "difference" a base to work from.

As this rationale for private schooling has displaced religious enthusiasm and ethnic loyalty, Australia has acquired a substantially secular, market-driven private school system governed by a dynamic of competition with the public schools, in which the presumed difference between private and public is central. This is a one-sided competition, since the organization and rationale of the public system has little reference to private education (with certain exceptions such as selective schools). It is not surprising that the initiative has been firmly on the "private" side.

The institutions. A market requires market institutions of two kinds: enterprises capable of competing, and an "exchange," a central place where transactions occur and market failure or success are registered.

In the commodification of education in Australia, "enterprises" existed in embryo in the form of schools founded by religious bodies, and in the commercial colleges, which provided some post-school vocational education (e.g. training for clerical work in "secretarial colleges"). A key part of the neo-liberal agenda has been to turn public education institutions themselves into "firms" that compete on a market. This has been largely achieved in the university sector and in the TAFE sector. It has been only partly achieved in the school sector.

A virtual "exchange" where market success and failure is registered is provided by matriculation-level exams, such as the Higher School Certificate in NSW. Though these are notionally measures of individual student performance, they can be tweaked into a "league table" of schools (e.g. numbers in the top 5000 students). This is a very imperfect register, from the point of view of the market agenda. It is focussed only at one level of education and is regionally specific. Therefore neo-liberals in education have given thought to how better competitive registers can be produced. At school level, national competitive testing seems the favoured option, and the far right government now in power federally is currently talking about a national matriculation exam. Such assessment mechanisms institutionalize social privilege. Important recent research on the process shows how selective and elite private schools craft strategies that allow them to dominate selection for elite levels of education (Teese and Polesel 2003).

It is the state, not the market, that provides the "exchange," the institutional mechanisms through which success and failure is registered. The market agenda does not eliminate the state from education, but it gives it a different role, that of guaranteeing the integrity of the market process. The ideal neo-liberal institution in Australia is the national competition commission, and the state will continue to perform a similar role in educational markets.

The need. Popular desire for education is historically variable, and does not always take the form of willingness to buy services in a market. For instance, the big postwar expansion of working-class demand for secondary education in Australia was mainly met by free state schools. Once a certain level of education has become expected, market-relevant need can be created by destroying free provision. This strategy is part of the market agenda; and to a dramatic extent has been accomplished in the TAFE sector where fees are now charged for all courses, a business orientation has taken over, and "access" programs for excluded groups have been shrunk.

The main mechanism for the creation of need, in contemporary Australia, is rather different. It centres on social difference and insecurity. In marketing their difference from public schools (and to a lesser extent from each other), the private schools call on their clientele's commonsense knowledge of social inequality and their anxiety in relation to economic and personal threats. In the early twenty-first century, three trends converge to produce this anxiety:

The first is structural change in the economy, which has made higher education crucial to the reproduction of wealth and to access to most elite careers and incomes. These changes mean that educational "failure" seems to have higher economic costs.

Second is the change loosely referred to as "globalization," which underpins neo-liberalism itself, and has unravelled postwar settlements and led to unpredictable economic turbulence. Crucially, globalization means higher levels of economic vulnerability in middle-class families as well as in the working class.

Third is a rising sense of personal insecurity, which is very well documented in Australian survey research around work/life balance (Pocock 2003). This anxiety seems especially focussed around women's lives, and is reflected in the marketing of segregated schools for girls. But it also includes a dimension of racial fear stimulated by the growing ethnic diversity of cities; and class fear in new forms, directed at "gangs," "underclass," "drug addicts," etc., i.e. threats to personal safety and comfort.

The private schools actively market themselves as solutions to these problems. They claim to offer "better schooling", providing advantages in learning that flow from a combination of traditional pedagogy, dedicated teachers, individualized attention and superior equipment. Whether there is any true technical advantage over state education is debatable, but appearance is enough for the purposes of the market. And the appearance of successful pedagogy is continuously created for private schools by the well-known effects of social class privilege in educational outcomes.

Just as important, the private school system responds to the growing culture of fear in contemporary market society. The private schools tacitly – but persistently – offer fee-paying parents a gated community for their children, in which turbulence, diversity and threat are held at a distance. This even becomes attractive to working-class parents, who as a result of the federal subsidies can now contemplate sending some children to the cheaper private schools (Connell 2003).

The imagery of private school advertising is telling in its insistence on order, calm, and uniformity. Outside the gated community is mess, disorder and impurity. Private school advertising cannot explicitly say that the children in public schools are dirty, lice-ridden, violent and ethnic, but the parents know what is meant by glossy photos of neat rows of uniformed children with clean white collars and well-brushed hair.

EFFECTS OF THE NEW-RIGHT AGENDA

What are the effects of privatization on educational processes? Contrary to the rhetoric of the market as an arena of freedom where "choice" guarantees diversity, the main tendency of commodified education is to reduce diversity, to converge on the most widely acceptable normative practice.

Normally the best marketing strategy will be to avoid niches, to avoid major risk (e.g. curriculum innovation), and to replicate the marketing successes of more established enterprises. So teachers in private schools are acutely conscious of what is being done in other private schools, and newer private schools tend to reproduce the culture, customs and language of the older ones, not only in pedagogy but down to such apparently minor details as style of uniform.

Similarly, in a partly-privatised university system, the pressure on the "weaker" institutions is to copy the more established universities as well as they can, in curriculum and style, rather than to become qualitatively different. Meanwhile the "stronger" institutions try frantically to distinguish themselves from the rest of the pack. In the wake of the neo-liberal restructuring that began in the late 1980s, the older and better-known Australian universities have formed themselves into an elite club called the "Group of Eight" ("G8", believe it or not). Their managers lobby the national government for special treatment, e.g. access to the bulk of national research funding, and appear to be making gains. There is a developing stratification of Australian higher education to a degree that has never existed before (Marginson 1997b).

The differentiation that occurs among schools, among colleges and among universities is not a deep diversity in educational philosophies, but a marginal differentiation in terms of market strength: demand for entry, ability to charge high fees, and prospects of growth. This differentiation is related to the enterprises' previous success in the "exchange" mechanisms, as well as to the effectiveness of their current marketing tactics.

The commodification of education has important effects on educational institutions and their workforces. There is a visible shift towards corporate methods of management. This includes: a shift of authority from teaching staff to managers; a heavier reliance on financial techniques of control; a greater focus on measurable outcomes rather than the performance of traditionally mandated tasks; a greater focus on corporate image and public relations; and a tendency to see other educational institutions as competitors rather than colleagues. (For a notable case study of the University of Melbourne see Cain and Hewitt 2004.)

The deepening commodification of education has very important consequences for the occupational cultures of teachers. There is an increasing distrust of teacher professionalism. This is very clearly shown by the current introduction of accreditation "Institutes" by state governments, which are new institutions of surveillance intended to control entry to teaching, scrutinize teacher education programs, and monitor teacher "performance."

Changes in organizational culture include the invasion of education by business ideology - we now have corporate "mission statements" in schools and universities, and "performance management" for staff, involving declaration of personal "goals" and measures of how well one has "achieved" them each year. Corporate-style managerial practices increasingly individualize the workforce, e.g. individualized salary bargaining, and individual measures of "performance." There is a tendency to modularize curricula to allow outsourcing, currently more marked in TAFE than schools. A counterbalance is the unionization of private school teachers, and the convergence between their unions and the unions of public school teachers.

There is also change at the level of curriculum and underlying values. As the privatisation agenda advances, educational institutions tend to shed the uncommodifiable. Those aspects of educational processes that do not produce competitive advantage will be de-emphasised by institutions performing in a market under competitive pressure. This includes areas of learning where the criterion is reaching a common competence, rather than competitive performance capable of being scaled (e.g. much of health education). It includes areas where the learning of one generally enhances the learning of others, so that the logic of competition does not apply (e.g. much of environmental education, and human relations). These moves have been rationalized by both Labor and Liberal governments as the pursuit of "rigour" and "excellence" in school education. The net effect has been a drift back towards a centrally controlled subject curriculum in the secondary schools, after decades in which schools had scope for teacher-based and more integrated curricula.

Schools are also under pressure to shed areas of work where a commitment of resources tends to lower the competitive performance or reputation of the institution. Examples are investing a lot of effort in teaching low achievers, or providing support for drug users – in short, teaching the "losers." In multiple ways, then, market pressures tend to narrow the aims of schooling.

As this also implies, the market agenda produces pressure against social justice in education. “Justice” as a concept is not part of the neo-liberal vocabulary of markets, choice, excellence and competition. (In the form of "retributive justice" it is part of the neo-conservative vocabulary, visiting punishment on deviants; this gives a punitive flavour to current talk about youth, drugs, teen pregnancy, and social turbulence of any kind - the consequence is more exclusion, not more inclusion.) To constitute schools as firms competing in a market, as we see in British research since the Thatcher era, is to set up incentives for "successful" schools to seek a middle-class clientele, while schools which do not do so, risk being residualized (Reay and Ball 1997, Gillborn and Youdell 2000).

Australian public schools, embedded in large bureaucratic systems, still offer a standard school provision to poor communities. We do not yet approach the level of economic inequality between school systems seen in the United States. Committed teachers in the public system are still able to do lively educational work in settings such as the "rust belt" schools described by Pat Thompson (2002), a famous principal in the South Australian system.

But they do so under increasing difficulties. De-industrialization, unemployment and insecure employment, and regressive tax "reforms" have led to widening gaps between rich and poor across Australia, and deepening difficulties in poor communities (Bryson and Winter 1999). It is clear from other research on disadvantaged schools, such as Dent and Hatton's (1996) ethnography of a primary school in Queensland, that teachers can be overwhelmed by the effects of poverty, racial tensions and social disruption in the community and the resulting difficulties of control and relevance in the school. And they are getting less and less institutional support for their efforts.

The highly innovative Disadvantaged Schools Program, supporting school-based programs since its foundation in the 1970s (Connell, White and Johnston 1991), was first narrowed to a "literacy" agenda and has now been closed down as a national program. "Multiculturalism", once a banner of openness and inclusion in our Anglo-dominated mono-lingual education system, is now officially disapproved. This particularly impinges on urban working-class schools, which often have multiple ethnic groups in their catchments. Prejudice against Arabic-speaking immigrant communities is now rising sharply, and there is no broad educational policy in response. A vigorous land rights movement from the 1970s was associated with an Aboriginal cultural revival and initiatives in Aboriginal education (Welch 1996, ch. 2). Racist attacks on targeted programs for Aboriginal communities – tacitly encouraged in the late 1990s by the national government as part of its very successful "wedge politics" strategy – have not ended Aboriginal education programs, but have stopped their growth and made them more cautious.

PROBLEMS OF THE PUBLIC SPHERE

To reject the gated community – the strategy of segregation, to name it plainly – is to embrace a principle of inclusiveness. This is the principle that state school systems have publicly embraced, and we need to think through its meanings and its difficulties.

Early Australian models of inclusive schooling come, ironically, from what now appears as the heartland of the new intolerance, the outback, in the form of the one-teacher primary school and the comprehensive community high school. The comprehensive model, the basis of secondary expansion from the 1950s to the 1980s, was supposed to achieve cohesion for the whole society by promoting social mixing in the schools.

This was assimilationist in ethnic terms. The language of instruction was always English, and initially very little recognition was given to diversity of culture and experience. It was also assimilationist in class terms. The old technical school system with its trade ethos and working-class clientele was eventually folded into the comprehensives, where technical education withered and an academic curriculum was hegemonic. The comprehensives offered working-class children a chance of academic promotion and access to professional jobs. But only a minority took that track. The comprehensives were generally streamed, in relation to the academic curriculum, and that meant de facto class selectivity inside the school, as well as the familiar and persistent social differentiation of schools based on the geography of catchment areas (Mukherjee 1996).

The comprehensive ideal was thus compromised, but it nevertheless provided a powerful image of inclusive education. The generation of young teachers who came into the system in the postwar boom decades often had a strong attachment to that ideal and worked hard to put it into practice. This comprehensivisation from below, following on the official comprehensivization from above, is a key moment in recent Australian education. The 1970s and 1980s saw a flowering of grassroots initiative to produce "relevant and meaningful" curricula, multicultural classrooms, school/community relations of new kinds, programs for girls, and indigenous education initiatives (Yates 1993, Welch 1996).

Inclusiveness is a policy that realizes a strong principle of educational justice. In discussions of "justice" it has been increasingly acknowledged that social justice not only concerns the distribution of material goods, but also concerns the distribution of respect or recognition. The segregationist strategy in education is precisely based on a denial of equal respect, on a desire to separate oneself or one's children from that which is disrespected. The idea of multicultural education, representing ethnic diversity not as an obstacle to schooling but as a source of richness for school life and curriculum, is a clear example of the principle of equality of respect.

The central difficulty with a principle of equal respect in education is that so much educational practice is devoted to establishing inequalities of worth. IQ tests, achievement tests, annual exams, first grade teams and second grade teams, streaming, selection, league tables, the Group of 8, the Ivy League, first- and second-class honours, pass v. failure – these are not marginal aspects of the education industry. Young people are unlikely to believe a rhetoric that says all are equally valued, when they know quite well the school honours a minority of "achievers" above all others.

The relationship between youth culture and education is important for a contemporary conception of public education, especially when we recognize that there is no one "youth culture" but a variety. There is commercial popular entertainment and marketing addressed to youth, there is avant-garde music, there is a range of subcultures (or subcultural fragments) from Goths to skateboarders to hip hop to rowing clubs, there are youth versions of ethnic cultures which have multiplied with the diversification of the population, there are also youth wings of social movements (notably environmentalism) and religions (White 1999).

Most of these cultural forms and subcultural scenes involve a conscious distancing from older generations. That's putting it mildly: the assertion of autonomy and independence often comes with expressions of distrust or angry refusal. The anger and distrust is there in the mass-mediated popular culture. It's also a matter of personal relations. Teachers in high schools now are the targets of a lot more angry and mistrustful speech than they were in earlier generations - an element in occupational stress and a problem in the maintenance of professional identity. Cultural change is also an element in pupil-to-pupil violence, an important (if often sensationalized) element in the creation of anxieties about schooling.

Private schools, by and large, deal with difficult youth subcultural issues by fencing them out. That's what the gated community is supposed to do for parents, the symbolic key being the fencing out of drugs. "Drugs" often serve as shorthand for the whole bothersome nexus of illicit substances, disorderly behaviour, sex, violence, hair dye and incomprehensible music.

Public schools can't fence out youth cultures, without fencing out half the people who need public schools. The problem for public education is a more demanding one. It is how to recognize personal worth across generational and cultural difference, and acknowledge young people's demand for autonomy, while also maintaining a teaching relationship with the whole age group, and keeping the schools safe places. The complexity of this task poses a greater challenge to develop professionalism among teachers than they are likely to encounter in private institutions.

An equally important dimension of youth culture is its deep diversity. The multiplicity of experiences, styles, ethnic and local backgrounds among children and youth requires from the schools a positive valuation of diversity, active engagement with multiple cultures and subcultures. The old multicultural policies were the merest shadow of what is needed. Yet current governments are retreating even from that mild acknowledgment of diversity.

Action in the public sphere encounters two difficult issues about the state. The first is the political success of neo-liberalism, which has meant a decline in the state's capacity to act as an arena of social decision-making, and a decline in the state's capacity to fund services such as education. There is a modest revival at present in support for the public sector, but a lot of damage has been done, including damage to teacher morale. In a "doing more with less" situation, managerial responses are likely to anger a workforce already under rising pressure. Work is required to renovate the very ideas of public interest and public service as something prior to the market.

The second issue is popular distrust of state institutions. This has old sources, since part of the history of the state is a history of repression and compulsion (in the language of the colonial Education Acts, "free, secular and compulsory"). Working-class families often encountered schooling as an offer they could not refuse from an impersonal, remote bureaucracy. In many situations this was accepted because the families valued what the schools were offering. But a social distance remained between working-class communities and state agencies, in Australia as in other countries (Reay 2001, Connell 2003). The resulting distrust has played into the privatisers' hands.

State institutions can only overcome this distrust by becoming more representative and responsive, in a word, more democratic. This applies to the schools and colleges themselves, and to the apparatuses that govern the system. Democratising institutions is not an easy thing to do. Some moves in this direction are little more than cosmetic, and the whole drift of managerialism is in the other direction. But it is a crucial issue in the renovation of public education. The experience of parent organizations should be an important source of ideas and methods.

PRINCIPLES OF PUBLIC EDUCATION

Despite all the pressures of the new right agenda, an impressive level of support for public education remains in the Australian community, as shown by a recent enquiry into public education in New South Wales – a joint initiative of the Teachers' Federation and the State government (Esson, Johnston and Vinson 2002). We do not have to abandon the field to the privatisers; there is still something to work with.

But an organizational revival of public education cannot be achieved just by political will; it also requires a renovation of ideas about public education. In this section, reflecting on the Australian experience, I suggest three main themes for this renovation. Public education is fundamentally inclusive; public education is based on a principle of equality; and public education is future-directed, or put another way, is based on social optimism rather than private fear.

Inclusion. The nineteenth-century creators of public schools spoke of "education for all." We should not forget how radical an idea that was, in an era when the upper classes thought of the populace as little better than animals. It is still a radical idea. In an inclusive system, you do not fence people out, and you do not price people out.

The inclusiveness of public education is based on an ethical principle – mutual responsibility. Through a public system, I share responsibility for your child and you share responsibility for mine. We share because we have a collective interest. The better education your child gets, the more my child benefits, and the more the whole society benefits. As everyone who has taught in a classroom knows, this is also a pedagogical principle. By and large, the better one pupil is learning, the better others will learn.

In a public education system, mutual responsibility is embodied in educational institutions - public schools and colleges, and the system of administration and teacher training behind them. The institutions are never perfect, but they are necessary for the ethical principle to have a continuing effect. Education on the scale of a whole society is a vast enterprise - simply in terms of the labour expended, it is the second-biggest industry in the country. Mutual responsibility is not casual charity; it is the principle behind the large-scale, continuing work of educators.

Inclusive education has another side, a principle of encounter. A public education system, because it provides for the whole society, must embrace diversity. Australian education systems have not done this very well in the past. We have too often written a monocultural curriculum and expected everyone to conform to it. But our schools today include Muslim, Christian and atheist, boy and girl, straight and gay, athletic and disabled, indigenous and new immigrant - and that's just the beginning of their complexity. Recognizing the deep diversity of modern societies requires a deep rethinking of curriculum and educational methods, an attention to curricular justice as well as equality of provision (Connell 1993).

Contemporary public education makes social diversity work for education, rather than treating diversity as an obstacle or a source of anxiety. Effective teachers design learning processes around the encounter between different experiences, cultures and perspectives. The diversity of educational needs can hardly be catered for in a single teaching/learning format. In the past, public systems have responded by specialization, e.g. the (now abolished) system of technical high schools. I think the path forward is more likely to be in creating centres that support a range of teaching/learning activities in a variety of formats - conventional classrooms, electronic learning networks, vocational workshops and laboratories, community-based programs, and so on. The cross-sectoral colleges now developing in NSW provide an example of this genre.

Equality. Public education is based on an underlying principle of equality. But "equality" is not a simple notion, as the philosophers tell us (Walzer 1983); equality in education has several dimensions. The first is a dimension of justice: public education embodies a community guarantee that all children, regardless of wealth, race or region, will have a decent basic education and access to advanced education. Thus an inclusive public system expresses the idea of equal rights in the sphere of education. Public education is linked here with the idea of common citizenship.

The second dimension concerns equal respect. The gated community attempts to keep out the rabble; public education denies that there is a rabble. Recognizing diversity as a resource, rather than a problem, implies that public schools respect the diverse experiences and cultures that their students bring into the classroom each day. This can be hard to do - given ethnic tensions, gender tensions, poverty, bullying, boredom, and other troubles of school life. But public schools do deal with these issues, most with competence and some with rousing success. In this, they are in line with modern philosophical discussions of equality and justice, which have come to emphasise issues of identity and respect (Young 1990).

Giving equal respect involves the curriculum. The competitive academic curriculum that has long reigned in Western education was created out of the experience and traditions of the 19th century European bourgeoisie. This curriculum still functions as a powerful machine for social filtering, and it is reinforced by every neo-conservative push for national testing, "league tables," and payment by results. To have a monocultural, socially exclusive curriculum dominating Australian schools is not just outdated - it is outright stupid, in a world of global diversity and increasing global interaction. Public schools, especially Victorian schools, have led the search for more inclusive curricula, valuing the experiences and using the resources of different social groups.

Thirdly, public education embodies equal provision. Our colonial predecessors built lovely public schools, real temples of education, in working-class suburbs and remote country towns as well as middle-class suburbs. They didn't do the same for Aboriginal or Chinese children - and Australia is still struggling with racism. Yet the principle of equal provision has been powerful, and remains important. It means offering education as generously to the most marginal, and the most troublesome, as to the most respectable and the most "gifted."

Making equal provision, society-wide, has traditionally meant state-supported education, and in modern conditions there is no other way of doing it. Tax revenues are the only way of supporting a large enough teaching workforce, while neutralizing (however imperfectly) the income inequalities of the market. This strategy is not trouble-free; the state is often distrusted, and is itself vulnerable to the market agenda. The answer to these problems is not to abandon the state, but to insist on more responsiveness, more democracy, within it.

Social optimism. Public education expresses not only the idea of mutual responsibility but also the idea of mutual aid. In helping each other, and each other's children, to learn, we are jointly building a society and a culture. In that sense, commitment to the public sector embodies a view of education based on hope, not on defensive fear.

Education is, in a larger view, one of the growth-points of culture. In the moment of transmission between generations, our culture is tested, adapted, and changed. It must change, as the world around us changes; but we have choices about how, about the directions we take forward. Change can be for the worse. The culture can be narrowed, made fearful or selfish. On the other hand cultural change can be expansive, exploratory, and enriching.

Public education assumes that we want constructive change. It represents the belief that through communication across diversity, we can build institutions that embody shared interests. In that very fundamental way, public education expresses the idea of democracy in education – since democracy (in the real sense) means constructive power in the hands of the people as a whole.

Democracy has to apply inside schools as well as outside. At all age levels, there are pedagogies that maximize active student involvement, student/teacher interaction, and shared authority in the learning process. This is the principle that should guide teaching and learning in a public education system. It means, at a basic level, we trust the learner. We don't assume learners have to be flogged on by endless tests, rewards and punishments. We look for joy in learning, for relevance in learning – and we acknowledge that kids will make mistakes in the course of their learning. A completely predictable program may be fine for a computer, but it's not education.

In a public education system, teachers too are citizens – not just hired hands – who are carrying a particular responsibility on behalf of other citizens. Public education also requires that, at a fundamental level, we trust the teacher. We give teachers respect as professionals. We provide the resources, the tools they need to do the job. We do not tie them up with "performance contracts," "teacher-proof packages," "external audits," or the other dismal fake-accountability mechanisms that the neo-liberals urge upon us.

This is not to claim that current methods of teaching are perfect. On the contrary, the traditional model of pedagogical authority is crumbling, and must change. For public education to flourish, there is need for a flourishing occupational culture in teaching – creating multiple connections among teachers and institutions, sharing methods and experience, developing professional pride. Teacher unions are a basis of teacher culture and are strategic participants in renovation. In-service education (sadly reduced during the funding squeezes) is a key method of renovation and can be a major asset for the public system. Direct communication with communities and families – the basis of real educational accountability – also needs resources and imagination.

Given the intensity of the pressures against public education in the last two decades, the wonder is not that heavily-subsidized private schools in Australia have increased their enrolments, and universities have gone overboard for fees – but that so much support for public education remains. To build constructively on that support requires conscious development that recognizes the implicit strengths of a public system, and responds better to the underlying needs that public education meets. It seeing the directions that the response to privatisation must develop, the Australian story – troubled as it is – may be of positive use to educators in other countries.

ACKNOWLEDGEMENTS

This paper originated in an address to the Forum on "Critical Visions and Education Policy," University of Technology, Sydney, 24 August 2001, subsequently published in *Education Links*, 2001/02, no. 63, 7-12. I am grateful to participants at that forum, and to colleagues and friends who have helped me to research and develop these ideas in the years since.

REFERENCES

Bryson, L and I. Winter. 1999. *Social Change, Suburban Lives: An Australian Newtown 1960s to 1990s*. Sydney, Allen & Unwin and Australian Institute of Family Studies.

Cain, J. and J. Hewitt. 2004. *Off Course: From public place to market place at Melbourne University*. Melbourne, Scribe.

Connell, R.W. 1993. *Schools and Social Justice*. Toronto, *Our Schools/ Our Selves*.

Connell, R.W. 2003. "Working-class families and the new secondary education." *Australian Journal of Education*, vol. 47 no. 3, 237-252.

Connell, R.W., V.M. White and K.M. Johnston. 1991. *'Running Twice as Hard': the Disadvantaged Schools Program in Australia*, Geelong, Deakin University.

Dent, J. N. & E. Hatton. 1996. "Education and poverty: An Australian primary school case study." *Australian Journal of Education*, vol. 40 (1), 46-64.

Esson, K., K. Johnston & T. Vinson. 2002. *Inquiry into the Provision of Public Education in NSW*. Sydney: Pluto Press Australia.

Gillborn, D. & D. Youdell. 2000. *Rationing Education*. Buckingham: Open University Press.

Lynch, K. & A. Lodge. 2002. *Equality and Power in Schools*. London: Routledge Falmer.

Marginson, S. 1997a. *Markets in Education.* St Leonards: Allen and Unwin.

Marginson, S. 1997b. "Competition and contestability in Australian higher education, 1987-1997." *Australian Universities Review*, vol. 40 no. 1, 5-14.

Mukherjee, Dev. 1996. *Regional Inequalities: Mapping the Geographic Locations of High Income, High Status Occupation and Outcomes from Education.* Sydney, Australian Centre for Equity through Education.

Pocock, B. 2003. *The Work/Life Collision: What work is doing to Australians and what to do about it.* Sydney, Federation Press.

Pusey, Michael. 1991. *Economic Rationalism in Canberra: A Nation-Building State Changes its Mind.* Cambridge, Cambridge University Press.

Reay, D. 2001. "Finding or losing yourself?: working-class relationships to education." *Journal of Education Policy*, vol. 16 (4), 333-346.

Reay, D. & S. J. Ball. 1997. "Spoilt for choice: The working classes and educational markets." *Oxford Review of Education*, vol. 23 (1), 89-101.

Rizvi, Fazal and Stephen Kemmis, 1987. *Dilemmas of Reform: An Overview of Issues and Achievements of the Participation and Equity Program in Victorian Schools 1984-1986.* Geelong, Deakin Institute for Studies in Education.

Teese, R. & J. Polesel. 2003. *Undemocratic Schooling.* Melbourne, Melbourne University Press.

Thompson, P. 2002. *Schooling the Rustbelt Kids.* Sydney: Allen & Unwin.

Walzer, M. 1983. *Spheres of Justice: A Defense of Pluralism and Equality.* New York, Basic Books.

Welch, A. 1996. *Australian Education: Reform or Crisis?* Sydney, Allen & Unwin.

White, R. 1999. *Australian Youth Subcultures: On the margins and in the mainstream.* Hobart, Australian Clearinghouse for Youth Studies.

Yates, L. 1993. "The Education of Girls: Policy, Research and the Question of Gender." *Australian Education Review* No. 35, Melbourne, ACER.

Young, I. M. 1990. *Justice and the Politics of Difference.* Princeton, Princeton University Press.

Labour's Transformation of the School System in England

RICHARD HATCHER AND BILL ANDERSON

It has been said that the greatest and most lasting achievement of Margaret Thatcher was the creation of New Labour. In school education it is certainly true that the policy of the Labour government has built on and extended the foundations laid by the Conservative governments of Thatcher and Major.[1] The decisive moment in Conservative education policy for schools was the 1988 Education Reform Act which inaugurated a dual strategy of increased marketisation, in the form of decentralisation of powers to school-based management at the expense of local education authorities, and increased centralised control in the form of a prescriptive national curriculum, national tests at age 7, 11, and 14, and the establishment of a new and punitive school inspection regime administered by the Office for Standards in Education (Ofsted).

The rationale for Conservative polices was three-fold. First, education needed to be made more efficient in terms of improving standards of pupil performance to meet labour market needs. The principal mechanism to achieve this was the creation of a quasi-market of competition among schools fuelled by an element of parental choice. The market was constructed and maintained by the state through the mechanisms of pupil-led funding and the publication of performance indicators, supplemented by state intervention, principally in the forms of financial incentives for success and Ofsted sanctions for failure. The stratification of the labour market required a stratified school system, and although the Conservatives had inherited a largely comprehensive system various mechanisms of social selection operated both between and within schools to ensure the reproduction of patterns of social class inequality, serving to maintain the educational privileges of the middle class on whom the Conservatives electorally depended. In addition the extension of the market principle into public service provision was presented as an extension of democracy, undercutting the dominance of bureaucratic local authorities and the sectoral interests of teacher unions.

Almost a decade later, in 1997, the Labour government came into office, and today, almost another decade after that, it is possible to look back on a period notable both for continuous education reform and continuity in the trajectory of policy. Four themes characterise Labour policy: increased state regulation of schooling, increased diversity of provision, the increasing role of the private sector, and the remodelling of the workforce.

INCREASED STATE REGULATION OF TEACHING

The first major difference between Labour government education policy and its predecessor's was a shift in the balance between the two drivers of change. Labour regarded competition in the school quasi-market as too weak a motor to transform the school system. The signals transmitted by the demand side were too weak, because parental choice of schools was not primarily governed by performance factors, and the supply side was too inflexible, because provision of school places was not responsive to parental demand. Improvement needed to be driven more forcefully by state intervention. This took two principal forms. Quantified improved performance targets were set for each school in core subjects and in attendance, which provided a new metric for Ofsted inspections. A new syllabus and pedagogy for the teaching of English and maths was imposed. The Literacy and Numeracy Strategies for primary schools were nominally voluntary but almost universally perceived as compulsory. For the first time, government prescribed not only what was to be taught but how it was to be taught, down to the level of sections of each hour-long daily lesson. The Literacy programme was later extended to the first three years of secondary school.

MORE DIVERSITY OF PROVISION

A key theme of Labour government education policy, as of the Conservatives', has been "choice and diversity." Labour has exacerbated the existing historical divisions within the British school system by attacking the notion of the comprehensive school (itself only partly achieved) and promoting different types of state schools. The most wide-ranging change has been the transformation of secondary schools into "specialist" schools, each specialising in a curriculum area, chosen from a government-approved menu, in addition to teaching the national curriculum. The rationale was that the creation of a diversity of provision corresponded to the diversity of pupil aptitudes, which was being suppressed by the alleged "drab uniformity" of the comprehensive school. The move was voluntary, but a substantial financial incentive has ensured that the vast majority of secondary schools are complying.

Any remaining hopes that comprehensive education could survive under New Labour were extinguished by the White Paper on 14-19 education, published in February 2005 (DfES 2005a). The core of the comprehensive ideal is a common school with a broad common core curriculum to the age of 16. The White Paper abandoned any pretence of this vision of education for all. From 14, while some will follow the traditional "academic" route leading to A Levels and a degree, the majority of young people will follow a narrow and diluted curriculum with a work-related element.

The White Paper defines "A broad and balanced compulsory curriculum until age 16" as follows: "The KS4 curriculum requires students to study English, maths, science, citizenship, RE and sex education; and to learn about careers and experience work-related and enterprise learning" (p71). There is no requirement to study the social sciences, the humanities, the arts or other languages. It is the educational equivalent of the national minimum wage – appropriately so, since that is what it will lead to for many. The justification for this impoverished curriculum is that in the rapidly changing knowledge economy the flexible adaptable future worker needs basic literacy and numeracy skills, appropriate personal skills, some vocational competences, and the right attitude. Everything else can be learnt on the job. Giving everyone a high quality comprehensive education is just needlessly inefficient and expensive.

The core of the White Paper curriculum is "work-related learning." From 14 years of age lower-achieving students will be part-time in school, part-time in Further Education colleges (providers of adult vocational education and training), and part-time in the workplace. This is a mechanism of social class selection. It is overwhelmingly young people from poorer backgrounds who will be channelled down this vocational route.

THE PRIVATE SECTOR AS AGENT OF CHANGE

Since the election of the Labour government in 1997 there has been a qualitative extension of the role of the private sector, in both for-profit and non-profit forms, in the provision of core educational services and policy delivery in the school system (Hatcher 2006). The rationale given by government is in terms of the private sector's contribution to efficiency and innovation. In 2001 Michael Barber, at the time the government's Chief Adviser on School Standards and Director of the Standards and Effectiveness Unit, posed the question:

> We need to ask ourselves from where the energy, knowledge, imagination, skill and investment will come to meet the immense challenge of educational reform over the next decade.
>
> For most of the twentieth century the drive for educational progress came from the public sector [...]. Towards the end of the twentieth century, as frustration with existing systems grew, this legacy was challenged by a growing vibrant private sector... (Barber 2001: 39)

The principal strategic function of the private sector in the school system is to "discipline and transform the old institutional sites of power" (Clarke and Newman 1997: 29). This enables us to explain the centrality in Labour education policy not only of for-profit business involvement but also the role of sponsorship on a non-profit basis by business interests and other agencies. It is therefore in this perspective of "re-agenting"(Jones 2004) that I want to examine first the role of for-profit companies and then the role of non-profit private involvement.

Almost every major government policy initiative has relied on private companies to translate it into practice, ranging from providing training for teachers in the national literacy and numeracy strategies to setting up the system of performance-related pay for teachers (Mahony, Hextall and Menter 2004), and most recently the decision of the National College for School Leadership to outsource the provision of its training programmes for headteachers.

Historically Local Education Authorities, the education departments of local municipal councils, have had an important role in the provision of education services to schools. Labour has continued the Conservative policy of eroding their powers and budgets. It has made clear, most recently in the 2005 White Paper, that the role of local authorities is to commission and broker services by private providers rather than to provide them themselves. The most extreme instances have been the compulsory transfer of a number of LEAs' entire provision to private companies as a result of failing an inspection by Ofsted.

The "delivery" of national policy initiatives and the provision of core services to LEAs and schools has proved a lucrative market for private companies, and has the additional function of incubating a British state-sponsored education-business sector capable of competing in the growing international education services market.

The huge growth of involvement by business on a for-profit basis in core educational processes has not extended to private companies taking over the running of state schools on a for-profit basis (with a handful of exceptions), even though this is permitted by government policy. There are three main reasons. It is not profitable enough. It is politically risky: likely to provoke popular opposition. And there is no evidence of demand either from parents or from employers of the future workforce that the state relinquishes its role in the direct provision of schooling. However, one of the most important innovations in Labour education policy has been the involvement on a non-profit basis of companies, business entrepreneurs and other private interests, mainly religious organisations, in the sponsorship of schools. Their function is to inject a new agency into the schools to align them with government agendas, driving change in school management and educational practices, including the promotion of a business-friendly culture and, in the case of religious sponsors, a Christian ethos. Sponsors have a range of motives, from philanthropy to the promotion of their company image and the desire to promote business values.

The first, and weaker, form of sponsorship concerned "specialist" schools. Secondary schools wishing to gain specialist status, now the overwhelmingly majority, have had first to obtain £50,000 worth of external sponsorship. Some has come from small donations, often from parents and other private individuals or small local businesses, some from large companies, including supermarkets, banks and manufacturing companies, allocating money from their "corporate social responsibility" budgets.

A second category of sponsorship concerns foundation schools. All primary and secondary schools can now apply for foundation school status, which gives them enhanced autonomy. They own their own assets, are the direct employers of staff and are their own admission authorities. They can also "forge a long-term partnership with an external sponsor, including business, charitable and faith sponsors" (DfES 2004, chap. 4. para. 23). The rationale is that an external sponsor "will be attractive to some weaker and 'coasting' schools as a source of new dynamism, as well as to more successful schools..." (DfES 2004, chap. 4. para. 23). Business sponsorship of foundation schools differs from sponsorship of specialist schools in several respects: it does not require a financial donation; it must be by means of a charitable trust; it is intended to be a long-term relationship; and it entitles sponsors to appoint governors.

The third form of sponsorship, by companies, individual business entrepreneurs, and religious and charitable organisations, is of Academies. Academies are a new category of publicly funded schools, many of them "newbuild," aimed at raising standards of attainment in socially deprived areas. They are set up under private school legislation, outside the LEA system, which gives them greater curricular autonomy than other state schools and the power to vary the pay and conditions of teachers. The government intends that 200 such schools should be established by 2010. Academies have private sponsors with much greater powers than those of specialist and foundation schools. In return for a one-off capital investment of £2 million, sponsors gain control of the school, through the transfer to them of ownership of the land and premises and through being able to appoint a majority of the governing body, with the remaining capital costs, and the running costs, met by the DfES. Tony Blair has said that he is committed to Academies because "an external sponsor [...] brings not only a financial endowment but also vision, commitment, and a record of success from outside the state school system" (quoted in Shaw 2004:1).

THE REMODELLING OF THE WORKFORCE

The transformation of the school requires the transformation of the workforce, from headteachers to classroom teachers and learning assistants.

A combination of three strategies is designed to ensure that headteachers are performing as reliable relays of government policy (Hatcher 2005). First, a battery of control mechanisms (targets, tests, Ofsted, etc) to lock schools – heads and teachers – into the government agenda. Secondly, the attempt to create a cadre of reliably "on-message" managers through the National College for School Leadership (NCSL). And thirdly, a set of specific powers for heads to manage teachers – performance management

The function of the NCSL is the ideological re-engineering of the culture of school management in order to secure not just the compliance of teachers with the government's agenda but their commitment to it. The vehicle is a model of "transformational leadership" imported from the world of business management. However, the ideological strategy is underpinned by a much more coercive mechanism: a new system of performance management of teachers by headteachers which determines promotion. To progress up the salary scales teachers must demonstrate that they have "grown professionally" and made "sustained and substantial progress," for which the criteria include pupil performance. This is potentially a powerful management tool in a context of below-inflation increases in teachers' nationally negotiated salaries.

The re-culturing of headteachers and the introduction of performance management has been complemented by the remodelling of the school workforce. The government's aim has been to break the monopoly of qualified teachers by allowing other categories of school workers to carry out their jobs. In January 2003 a "national remodelling agreement" was signed between the government, national employers' organisations, trades unions representing adults working in education and five of the six teacher trades unions. Only the largest teachers union, the National

Union of Teachers, opposed it. The agreement allowed "teaching assistants," classroom support staff without teaching qualifications, to take whole classes to cover for absent teachers, relieving other teachers of the responsibility. Training and rises in salary were promised to teaching assistants to close the gap with teachers. In July 2003 regulations were drafted to give headteachers discretionary powers to employ staff without teaching qualifications to teach the non-statutory parts of the National Curriculum. In fact, the regulations stipulated that the only member of staff who had to be a qualified teacher was the head. This was accepted by all the teacher unions, with the exception of the NUT, as a way of giving teachers time away from their classes to "plan, prepare and assess" (PPA).

This package of measures convinced the union leader signatories that they were in the driving seat of the modernisation programme. Their incorporation into the government's agenda, in the name of "social partnership," was confirmed in 2004 when, as participants in the government's Remodelling Implementation Group they accepted the proposal to restructure the payments paid to teachers for responsibilities additional to their class teaching duties which would result in actual salary reductions for thousands of teachers within three years. The proposal also allowed support staff without teacher qualifications to take on pastoral and behavioural roles, breaking with a fundamental tenet of pedagogy in the UK that the teacher is responsible for the development of the whole child.

The short-term gain for teachers is some increase in PPA time, but it is at the expense of an overall reduction in the global salary bill and the creation of a two-tier workforce, entailing a future reduction in the number of qualified teachers employed in schools.

THE UNRAVELLING OF LABOUR'S "STANDARDS AGENDA"

For the past eight years the Labour government has been able to rebuff criticism of its education policies with the claim that they are justified by the rise in standards. A number of recent research reports have challenged this claim.

The most far-reaching study is *Standards in English schools: changes since 1997 and the impact of government policies and initiatives*, a report by Peter Tymms, Robert Coe and Christine Merrell published in April 2005. This is their conclusion:

> For both the end of primary schooling and the end of compulsory secondary education the gain in attainment over nearly a decade is small. In technical terms they both amount to an Effect Size of about 0.2. In the educational research literature many tightly controlled intervention studies have been shown to have much greater Effect Sizes and an Effect Size of 0.2 is not regarded as of great moment.
>
> Impact of Initiatives: Evaluation and monitoring
>
> The gains have been modest but the efforts have been massive. Hundreds of millions of pounds spread across hundreds of initiatives have been invested. One has to ask if the money could have been better spent. It is our opinion that many changes that were put into place without sufficient evidence of their effectiveness before they were released into schools. […] Of the hundreds of initiatives put in by the British Government very, very few, could be said to have a strong evidence-base and in no case to our knowledge has their impact in situ been rigorously evaluated. (Tymms, Coe and Merrell 2005: 21)

Furthermore, as a report by the Statistics Commission (2005) confirmed, a large part of the improvement in test scores is due to teachers "teaching to the test".

Social inequality in schooling

The government's overall aim has been to raise standards of pupil attainment. But even if overall test scores rise, educational inequality is not necessarily reduced, as the government has belatedly acknowledged in its *Five year strategy for children and learners* (DfES 2004):

> 20. […]Those from higher socio-economic groups do significantly better at each stage of our system than those from

lower ones – indeed [...] socio-economic group is a stronger predictor of attainment than early ability.

21. In general, though, those that do well early do even better later in life, while those that do not perform well fall further behind; and the chances of breaking out of this cycle of underachievement reduce with age.
22. Those who do better than average at age 7 are more than twice as likely to get qualifications at degree level by the age of 25 than those who performed poorly at 7. Results for 11 year-olds show an even starker picture – over 85 percent of 11 year-olds that do not reach the expected level for their age will not get five good GCSEs at age 16. [...]
23. This is not simply a case of the system recognising and labelling learners' innate levels of ability. The gap between the best and worst performers in our system actually widens as they go through education; and it is both significantly wider and more closely related to socio-economic status in this country than elsewhere. (DfES 2004, chapter 1)

Patterns of social inequality are the result not just of the profound social inequalities in British society, themselves sustained by government policies, but also of the government's own education policies. The government's claim that "diversity and choice" are the best way both to raise standards and to reduce inequality is contradicted by evidence from the PISA study comparing school student attainment in a number of countries (OECD/Unesco, 2003). The UK performs well overall but has one of the largest attainment gaps between rich and poor students in the developed world. The PISA report shows that comprehensive school systems are more effective at reducing inequality. It praises Finland, which performed best in the study, for its comprehensive system and for giving teachers a high degree of responsibility and autonomy. Andreas Schleicher, head of the OECD's educational indicators and analysis division, says there are no advantages to selection. "The trade-off between quality and equity does not exist in reality." This finding contradicts the Labour government's policies of diversity of types of schools coupled with selection by parental choice and, overtly or covertly, by schools themselves, which tends to create an even more hierarchical school system and to reinforce patterns of social segregation, because middle class parents have the social capital to be able to "play the system" more successfully.

Government policy tends to reinforce social inequality in a more subtle way within the classroom. It conceptualises children's learning in terms of scores, levels and targets, and this has had a profound effect on how teachers conceptualise the abilities of children. This is the theme of Hart and her co-authors in their book *Learning without Limits*:

> …the act of categorising young people by ability reifies differences and hardens hierarchies, so that we start to think of those in the different categories as different kinds of learners with different minds, different characteristics and very different needs. (Hart *et al* 2004, p. 29).

Assessment has become central to the teacher's role, and its primary purpose is selection, not the diagnosis of learning needs.

> One important way in which the fixed ability template affects teachers' thinking is that it creates a disposition to accept as normal, indeed inevitable, the limited achievement of a significant proportion of the school population. (Hart *et al* 2004, pp. 28-9).

Government policy has been to encourage teachers to make different provision for different pupils on the basis of their perceived ability, resulting in a differentiated curriculum which becomes a process of social selection through negative discrimination – giving less to those who have less – locking working class pupils into a spiral of increasing inequality of attainment.

"Social inclusion" is a theme of government education policy, and a number of policy initiatives have been aimed at "raising standards" in socially disadvantaged areas. The three major initiatives have been Sure Start, Excellence in Cities and the Academies programme. However the evidence is that they have had little effect in reversing the effects of social inequality and government economic and education policies which tend to reinforce it. A study of Sure Start concluded that "The data indicated very little change over the years measured in response to government initiatives" (Merrell and Tymms 2005: 13). Excellence in Cities has put substantial extra funding into schools in socially deprived areas. A recent evaluation carried out by the National Foundation for Educational Research for the DfES found some limited improvements but no impact on GCSE grades at age 16 (Kendall et al. 2005). The most recent policy to target standards in socially deprived areas is Academies. A study by Gorard (2005) of the first three Academies, which opened in 2002, and their predecessor schools concludes that pupil attainment has improved in only two of them and that it is largely due to a change in social composition, attracting more middle-class students.

> Are Academies a solution to the perennial problem for school improvers? Do they deliver superior educational outcomes without changing the nature of their student intake? The answer, on the evidence available here, has to be 'no.' (p375)

> Sleight-of-hand school improvement involves schools changing the nature of their intake, often as an unintended outcome of a change in admission procedures, and then claiming that an ensuing rise in test scores is due to an improvement in teaching or management. The early Academies show signs of already doing this. (p376)

The levelling out of the initial improvements, albeit exaggerated, of the prescriptive "standards agenda" represents something of a crisis in the government's perspectives for education which it has sought to resolve with two new policy developments. The first has been an attempt to give the impression of a certain relaxation in centralised control, allowing some increase in freedom for teachers to try new approaches, exemplified by the title of a primary school policy document "Excellence and Enjoyment" and the promotion of "creativity" in learning. However, teachers are conscious that innovation and experiment is risky while the battery of performance controls (targets, test scores, Ofsted inspections, performance management, etc) remain in place.

MORE SPONSORS, MORE COMPETITION, MORE INEQUALITY – BLAIR'S LAST ACT?

The second new development, the White Paper *Higher Standards, Better Schools For All: More choice for parents and pupils* (DfES 2005b), represents a further ratcheting up of the neo-liberal agenda. When New Labour came to power it introduced new measures of central control over the school system, believing that Thatcherite marketisation was not a powerful enough motor of change. Now it concludes that state intervention is not enough. According to the then cabinet office secretary John Hutton (subsequently promoted to Work and Pensions Minister), speaking to the neo-liberal Brookings Institute in Washington in October 2005,

> We needed to drive greater challenge into the system, and that could not be entirely reliant upon target setting and performance management from the centre. It does involve greater contestability, the opening up of these monolithic structures from across the private, voluntary and social enterprise sector. This has proved to be our biggest political challenge. The expected opposition from the trade unions and the professional interest groups was predictable and it has happened. (quoted in Wintour 2005: 12)

"Contestability" is the current euphemism for competition. Two mechanisms of change need to be stepped up. One is more marketisation in the form of breaking up the LEA system into individual competing schools driven by consumer choice by parents and league tables of performance. Marketisation tends to reinforce middle-class advantage, and this is the predictable and intended consequence of the White Paper, cementing Labour's electoral strategy.

The other mechanism, extending the experience of specialist and foundation schools and, in particular, Academies, is the role of external sponsors in driving change. The White Paper says that "At the heart of this new vision are Trust schools." This is a new category of state school with external sponsors who "will harness the external support and a success culture, bringing innovative and stronger leadership to the school, improving standards and extending choice. We will encourage all primary and secondary schools to be self-governing and to acquire a Trust." (DfES 2005b: 24-5)

Trusts are non-profit bodies with charitable status which can appoint a majority of a school's governing body and thus control the school (though even where the Trust only chooses to have minority representation it would clearly exercise significant influence). Sponsors could be private companies, the churches and other religious organisations, and charitable organisations, including those set up by business entrepreneurs. Companies which have already expressed an interest are KPMG and Microsoft. (Microsoft already sponsors 100 specialist schools.) Sponsorship by religious interests seems certain to be a big growth area, encouraged by Blair's promotion of "faith" schools. The White Paper encourages federations of schools, and this may prove attractive to entrepreneurial headteachers and school governing bodies which want to establish a "branded" chain of sponsored state schools, exemplified by Thomas Telford school, which has used its profits, amounting to several million pounds, from selling examination courses online to sponsor some 46 specialist schools and two Academies.

The White Paper also contains other pro-market policies: in particular, to allow schools to set their own admissions policies, thus opening the door to more social selection. This proposal provoked the largest rebellion by Labour MPs since the invasion of Iraq, forcing the government to retreat. However, their opposition did not extend to Trust schools. Nevertheless, it is difficult at this stage to predict the extent to which schools will take the Trust option, given that there is no statutory compulsion – itself an indication of how politically risky the government senses is this further encroachment of private interests in the school system. Nor are there any direct financial incentives from government. And, as John Dunford, general secretary of the Secondary Heads Association, has said, "The freedoms being offered in the white paper are largely an illusion" (quoted in White and Taylor 2005b: 12). However, there are two powerful levers for moving schools to adopt Trust status. One is market pressure. In a competitive local schools market Trust status, with a prestigious business or religious sponsor, may be seen as a key advantage in terms of parents' perceptions. It may only need one school in a local area to go for Trust status to start a domino effect. The other lever is the ability of the government to use the mechanism of Trust status to force "failing" schools to be taken over by external sponsors, either business interests or a federation of schools run by an executive "super head." In many cases these will become vocational schools supplying work-related learning and training to meet local labour market needs.

OPPOSITION AND RESISTANCE

Many of Labour's education policies have provoked widespread opposition, and not only from teachers; among them the SATs tests and league tables of school performance, the dismantling of comprehensive education, the various forms of privatisation, the prescriptive National Literacy Strategy, the quasi-market of competing schools, aspects of remodelling the workforce, and most recently the White Paper. But opposition has seldom been translated into active resistance. To understand why, we have to situate the politics of education in the wider political context. After the defeat of the miners' strike in the mid-1980s by the Thatcher government, the leadership of the trade union movement adopted a strategy of waiting for a Labour government. The New Labour project has created many tensions with the trade union movement, but the dominant strategy of the union leaderships remains one of "social partnership" with government, seeking small concessions from government in exchange for eschewing industrial action. The current political period exhibits something of a paradox. There is a relatively high level of active political opposition to Labour government policies, exemplified by the largest anti-war demonstration in British history, while at the same time union action in the workplace is at a low ebb. No union has been willing to use its collective strength to confront the government, and certainly not the National Union of Teachers, the largest teachers union, which itself suffered a decisive defeat of its strike campaign over pay at the same time as the miners' strike and has not taken national industrial action since then.

Broadly speaking, there are two currents of opposition to Labour education policy, pursuing two somewhat different strategies. One is historically based in the movement for comprehensive education, which was partially achieved in the 1960s. It comprises a number of pressure groups inside and around the Labour party, and their principal strategy has been, and remains, to influence Labour party and, when in office,

Labour government policy. The price it chooses to pay in return for the hoped-for influence in the corridors of power is to avoid any connection with militant trade unionism. This strategy is in something of a crisis since, with the exception of some compromises over the White Paper, the Labour leadership has felt able to completely disregard this current, exemplified by its refusal to complete the comprehensive education reform by abolishing the remaining 160 or so selective "grammar" schools.

The other current of opposition is based in the National Union of Teachers. The failure of the leadership's preferred strategy of "social partnership" to assuage the relentless attacks on teachers' pay and conditions of work, let alone to extract any significant concessions, has resulted in a growth in the influence of the left within the union, organised in two broad, unofficial but open tendencies. Currently the left is playing a leading role in local strikes by teachers over aspects of remodelling and in a number of vigorous local campaigns by parents and teachers against Academies, which represent the highest level of popular activity in school education for many years (Hatcher and Jones 2006). What is absent is an over-arching national strategy of action. However, for many years now the left has dominated the annual union conference, and it has the realistic perspective of becoming a majority of the union leadership in the next two or three years. The emergence of a new "class struggle" leadership in the NUT parallels similar developments taking place in several other unions outside education, and would represent a fundamental change in the education landscape.

NOTES

[1] This chapter focuses on England. The school systems in Scotland, Wales and Northern Ireland are different for historical reasons, and devolution of government in recent times has strengthened their ability to resist elements of the New Labour agenda.

REFERENCES

Barber, M. (2001) High expectations and standards for all, no matter what: creating a world class education service in England. In M. Fielding (ed) *Taking Education Really Seriously: Four Years' Hard Labour*. London: RoutledgeFalmer.

Clarke, J. and Newman, J (1997) *The Managerial State*. London: Sage.

DfES (Department for Education and Skills) (2004) *Five year strategy for children and learners*. London: HMSO.

DfES (Department for Education and Skills) (2005a) 14-19 *Education and Skills*. London: HMSO.

DfES (Department for Education and Skills) (2005b) *Higher Standards, Better Schools For All: More choice for parents and pupils*. London: HMSO.

Gorard, S. (2005) Academies as the 'future of schooling': is this an evidence-based policy? *Journal of Education Policy* 20 (3) 369–377.

Hart, S., Dixon, A., Drummond, M. J. and McIntyre, D. (2004) *Learning without Limits*, Maidenhead: Open University Press.

Hatcher, R. (2005) The distribution of leadership and power in schools. *British Journal of Sociology of Education*, 26 (2) 253-267.

Hatcher R (2006) Privatisation and sponsorship: the re-agenting of the school system in England. *Journal of Education Policy* (forthcoming).

Hatcher, R. and Jones, K. (2006) Researching Resistance: campaigns against Academies in England. (In submission)

Jones, K. (2004) A New Past, an Old Future: New Labour Remakes the English School. In D. L. Steinberg and R. Johnson (eds) *Blairism and the War of Persuasion*. London: Lawrence and Wishart.

Kendall, L., O'Donnell, L., Golden, S., Ridley, K, Machin, S., Rutt, S., McNally, S., Schagen, I., Meghir, C., Stoney, S., Morris, M., West, A., and Noden, P. (2005) *Excellence in Cities: The National Evaluation of a Policy to Raise Standards in Urban Schools 2000-2003*. London: DfES.

Mahony, P., Hextall, I. and Menter, I. (2004) Building dams in Jordan, assessing teachers in England: a case study in edu-business, *Globalisation, Societies and Education* 2 (2) 277-296

Merrell, C. and Tymms, P. (2005) 'The impact of early interventions and pre-school experience on the cognitive development of young children in England'. Paper presented at AERA Annual General Meeting, Session 70.091, Montreal, April. Available at http://www.pipsproject.org/PDFs/ImpactOfPreSchool.pdf [Accessed 15 December 2005].

OECD/Unesco (2003) 'Literacy skills for the world of tomorrow – further results from Pisa 2000', *Education and Skills* no. 5, pp. 1-392.

Shaw, M. (2004) Blair seeks to relax rules for academy bids, *Times Educational Supplement* 2 April, p1.

Statistics Commission (2005) *Measuring Standards in English Primary Schools*. London: Statistics Commission. Available at http://www.statscom.org.uk/media_pdfs/reports/023%20-%20Measuring%20Stds%20in%20English%20schools.pdf [Accessed 15 December 2005].

Tymms, P., Coe, R., and Merrell, C. (2005) *Standards in English schools: changes since 1997 and the impact of government policies and initiatives.* Durham: CEM Centre, University of Durham. Available at http://www.civitas.org.uk/pdf/Tymms_SundayTimes_v03.pdf [Accessed 15 December 2005].

White, M. and Taylor, M (2005) Blair sweeps aside critics of school reform. *The Guardian* 25 October, p1.

Wintour, P. (2005) Blair's public service crusade. *The Guardian* 25 October, p12.

Leaving Public Education Behind: The Bush Agenda in American Education

STAN KARP

It is a measure of how far the right is reaching that the left today finds itself defending the very existence of public education from the forces of privatization, commercialization, and even federal policy.

Just four years after the 1996 Republican Presidential candidate Bob Dole campaigned on a platform of abolishing the Department of Education, the Bush Administration came into office with a massive expansion of the federal role in education as its number one domestic priority. This time, however, the goal was not to extend the federal government's historic role as a promoter of educational access and equity, but to replace it with a conservative agenda of punitive high stakes testing, privatization, and market "reforms."

ROOTS OF NCLB

The euphemistically named Bush education bill, the *No Child Left Behind Act*, was passed in December 2001 with overwhelming Republican and Democratic support, (381-41 in the House, 87-10 in the Senate).[1] While the bipartisan coalition that supported passage of NCLB has long since fragmented, its initial creation reflected the bill's merger of the corporate-centrist agenda of standards and tests with the right's agenda of vouchers ("choice") and privatization. Like most effective political strategies, NCLB rhetoric also spoke to real concerns held by large numbers of people, particularly those that have been badly served by public education. These concerns included persistent racial gaps in student achievement, a lack of institutional accountability, and seemingly intractable school failure in low-income communities of color. These very real problems have provided a platform for school reformers of all shapes and sizes to posture as champions of the underserved and underprivileged.

For Bush, education reform has always been an "outreach" issue. He came into office as a dubiously-elected President with historically low levels of support among African Americans and a well-deserved anti-poor, pro-business image. Education is one of the few areas that allow a Republican President to posture, however disingenuously, as an ally of poor people of color. By focusing on the lowest performing schools and the racial dimensions of the achievement gap (e.g. the "soft bigotry of low expectations"), Bush gave his education rhetoric an edge and an urgency it would otherwise lack. However, he has used this rhetoric, both as Texas Governor and later as President, to frame policy proposals that have reinforced the "hard bigotry" of institutional racism in education, for example, by promoting higher dropout rates and perpetuating funding inequities. (Combining rhetorical concern for the victims of inequality with policies that perpetuate it may be an operative definition of "compassionate conservatism.")

But the common ground that really gave birth to NCLB was the standards movement. And this traces back to the first "Education President," George Bush the elder, and to the Governors' Education Summits promoted by then-Arkansas Governor Bill Clinton. The standardize and test strategy, now enshrined in NCLB and raised to new and absurd heights by the "adequate yearly progress" formulas that NCLB is currently imposing on every school in the nation, was made possible by a decade of promoting standards and tests as the key to school improvement.

Today, standardized curricula imposed through ever-more suffocating layers of standardized testing have become the primary instruments of mainstream, corporate-sponsored school reform. Putting aside for the moment their limited utility in school improvement processes, standards and tests have become strategic tools used to impose external political and bureaucratic agendas on local schools and districts. The standards and testing movement has done even more than the privatization schemes of the voucher supporters to move school power away from teachers, classrooms, schools and local districts, and to put it in the hands of state and national politicians.

Such uses of standards and testing in the service of larger policy objectives is exactly what a number of conservative strategists have been proposing for years. As Nina S. Rees, a former Heritage Foundation researcher who is now an official in the Department of Education, wrote before Bush took office, "Standards, choice, and fiscal and legal autonomy in exchange for boosting student test scores increasingly are the watchwords of education reform in America. The principle can be used in programs that apply to whole districts as well as entire states. Importantly, it lays the groundwork for a massive overhaul of education at the federal level in much the same way that welfare reform began."[2]

A CURRICULUM COUNTER-REVOLUTION

This overhaul, codified in NCLB, is now underway and has schools across the country reeling as the law's impact unfolds in numbing bureaucratic detail. NCLB requires all states to adopt curriculum standards and enforce them with annual testing in grades 3 through 8 and once again in grades 9-12. (Bush recently proposed extending annual testing through high school.) Estimates are that over 90% of the nation's public schools will eventually find themselves facing sanctions on the narrow basis of annual test scores and unreachable performance targets. The scheme uses achievement gaps among up to 10 different student groups to label schools as "failures," without providing the resources or support needed to eliminate them. NCLB includes an unfunded mandate that by 2014, 100 percent of all students, including special education students and English-language learners, must be proficient on state tests. Schools that don't reach increasingly unattainable test score targets face an escalating series of sanctions up to and including possible closure and the imposition of private management on public schools.[3]

The sanctions that NCLB imposes have no record of success as school improvement strategies, and in fact are not educational strategies at all. They are political strategies designed to bring a kind of market reform to public education. They will do little to address the pressing needs of public schools, but they will create a widespread perception of systemic failure, demoralize teachers and school communities, and erode the common ground that a universal system of public education needs to survive.

NCLB is also promoting a kind of curriculum counter-revolution, narrowing the range of what is taught to what is tested, and advancing pseudo-scientific justifications for particular brands of scripted, pre-packaged, commercially-produced instructional materials. In the process, standardization is squeezing out more democratic and pluralistic educational visions.

Multicultural education, in particular, has been a casualty. The social movements of the 60s and 70s, and the shifting demographics of public school populations (more than 40% are now students of color) have been pushing schools to more accurately reflect in their curricula the changes occurring in their classrooms. Social movements for the rights of working people, African Americans, women, disabled people, gays and lesbians, and others have forced changes in cultural sensibilities and federal and state law. Several decades of academic scholarship have revised traditionally narrow versions of literature and history study. Lumbering school bureaucracies, which have rarely been on the cutting edge of change, were finally trying to catch up by taking a closer look at their textbooks, course outlines, and bulletin boards.

Progressive forces tried to build this movement for multicultural education into more substantive democratic and antiracist efforts. They made some significant, if modest progress, for example encouraging educators to "rethink Columbus" during the Quincentennial in the mid 1990s, and revising traditional reading lists and history units to include previously silenced voices.

But as the standards and testing regime spread, multicultural curriculum reform has increasingly been replaced with standardized, and sanitized, versions of "what everyone must know." This standardization is justified as a necessary response to persistent school failure, and it supporters have been adept at using educational inequality and academic achievement gaps to frame such policies.

But this has not made simplistic, standardized approaches to "systemic" reform any more effective in addressing the staggering inequality that is reflected in the test score gaps. Instead, at the level of curriculum and instructional practice, it has given rise to a regimented, almost militarized, approach to "standards-based, data-driven reform" that has had striking consequences, especially for poor, urban schools.

Jonathan Kozol writes extensively about this in *The Shame of America: the restoration of apartheid schooling in America.* (1995) (The book, in part, is an update of Kozol's *Savage Inequalities* (1991) which detailed inequities in education funding.) Kozol describes the instructional impact of the standards and testing regime:

> An expansive academic industry has now evolved around the elements of what is known generically as 'standards-based reform'... new systems of incentive, and new modes of castigation, which are termed 'rewards and sanctions,' have emerged. Curriculum materials that are alleged to be aligned with governmentally established goals and standards and particularly suited to what are regarded as 'the special needs and learning styles' of low-income urban children have been introduced. Relentless emphasis on raising test scores, rigid policies of nonpromotion and nongraduation, a new empiricism and the imposition of unusually detailed lists of named and numbered 'outcomes' for each isolated parcel of instruction, an oftentimes fanatical insistence upon uniformity of teachers in their management of time, an openly conceded emulation of the rigorous approaches of the military and a frequent use of terminology that comes out of the world of industry and commerce – these are just a few of the familiar aspects of these new adaptive strategies....and although most educators speak of these agendas in broad language that sounds applicable to all, it is understood that they are valued chiefly as responses to perceived catastrophe in deeply segregated and unequal schools.[4]

IMPACT OF THE TESTING REGIME

This obsessive over-reliance on test-driven standardized instruction in the name of accountability is more than bad education policy. It is a political effort to push other more democratic approaches to school improvement aside. When schools become obsessed with standards and test scores, they often narrow the focus of what teachers do in classrooms and limit their ability to serve the broader needs of children and their communities. High-stakes exams encourage schools to adopt developmentally inappropriate practices for younger children, special needs students and English Language Learners in an effort to "get them ready for the tests." They push struggling students out of school and promote tracking. Overuse of testing can also encourage cheating scandals and makes schools and students vulnerable to inaccurate and, at times, corrupt practices by commercial testing firms. Testing diverts attention and resources from more promising, and sometimes most costly, school improvement strategies, like smaller schools and class size, multicultural curriculum reform, and collaborative, school-based professional development. Instead of investing in the professional capacity of teachers and schools, resources are channeled to test and textbook publishers (often one and the same) and authority is moved away from classrooms and teachers.

Standards and testing, especially as they have been implemented in recent decades, are not designed to make schools accountable to students, their families, or their communities, or even to educators. They are designed to increase the ability of external political and educational bureaucracies to impose top-down, "systemic" control on curriculum, instructional practice, and other matters of educational policy. Even when the goals do include real educational accountability, standardized tests are of limited value. According to some researchers, 70% of the change in year-to-year test scores, which forms the basis for NCLB's "accountability system," can be caused by random fluctuation – things like variations in transient student population or statistical error in the tests themselves. They concluded that NCLB's testing system "cannot tell the difference between a learning gain and random noise."[5]

Assessing the effectiveness of a particular school or program requires multiple measures of academic performance, including classroom observations, portfolios of student work, and sustained dialogue with real teachers and students, as well as a range of indicators from attendance and drop-out rates to graduation rates and post-graduation success, measures of teacher preparation and quality, surveys of parent participation and satisfaction and similar evaluations. Legitimate assessment strategies would also measure "opportunity to learn" inputs and equity of resources so that the victims of educational failure were not the only ones to face "high stakes" consequences.

The push for standardization is often accompanied by rhetoric about "high expectations" and "college preparation for all." The need to "compete in the global economy," and "prepare for the high tech future" is also regularly invoked. This rhetoric puts a veneer of "equity" and "national urgency" on the testing regime and, resonates with concerns held by many who care about schools and children. But it also papers over the growing gap between "world class educational standards" and the levels of preparation and support that many struggling students bring with them to school. According to the Alliance for Excellent Education, typically half of all students entering a high-poverty high school read at a seventh-grade level or below.[6] Without dramatic changes in how schools function and the resources available to them, linking "higher expectations" and high-stakes tests in an increasingly regimented sorting system will lay the basis for new and severe forms of tracking. The standards and testing regime may end up slightly expanding the strata of students prepared for college and careers after high school, while pushing much larger numbers of students out of schools completely and into the streets, the unemployment lines and the prisons.

SOME GAPS COUNT MORE THAN OTHERS

Moreover, while inequality in test scores is one narrow indicator of school performance, test scores also reflect other inequalities that persist in the larger society and in schools themselves. About 12% of white children live in poverty, while over 30% black and Latino children live in poverty. The richest 1% of households has more wealth than the bottom 95%. Students in low-income schools, on average, have thousands of dollars less spent on their education than those in wealthier schools. About 14% of whites don't have health insurance, but more than 20 percent of blacks and 30%of Latinos have no health insurance. Unemployment rates for blacks and Latinos are nearly double what they are for whites.[7]

In October, 2003, the Educational Testing Service released a study on the achievement gap concluding, "The results are unambiguous. In all 14 factors, the gaps in student achievement mirror inequalities in those aspects of school, early life, and home circumstances that research has linked to achievement."[8]

Yet we do not hear NCLB's supporters demanding an end to this kind of inequality. Nor do we hear the federal government saying that all crime must be eliminated by 2014 or the police will be privatized, all citizens must have good health care or we will shut down the health care system.

APPEALS TO PARENTS

Many organized groups representing parents and people of color have seen through NCLB's rhetorical promises and joined efforts to reform or repeal it. The Boston-based advocacy group FairTest has spearheaded a reform campaign that has won support from the NAACP, the Children's Defense League and the Hispanic advocacy organization, Aspira.[9] A recent report on "community organizing for school reform in the era of NCLB" summed up the concerns of such equity advocates: "NCLB is sucking the oxygen out of any broader national debate over what to do about public education, especially in major urban centers…[it] is built on a rhetorical stage of equity, high standards, and accountability that is widely supported by communities, parents, and progressive school reformers. But, beneath its red, white, and blue bunting, the frame of *No Child Left Behind* is ominously shaky. Parents, organizers, and their allies suspect the motives of many of the law's architects, question its relevance to improving what happens in classrooms of low-income students, and fear its capacity for further stressing school systems that are already imploding."[10]

At the same time, there are others that have bought into NCLB's promises. While they may have doubts about the law and its sponsors, significant numbers of poor parents, some with generations of negative experience with public schools, are less interested in exposing NCLB, than they are in finding ways to use it to put pressure on schools to improve. In NCLB, they see public reporting mandates that put a focus on racial gaps in student achievement, demands that schools respond to the these gaps effectively or face penalties, and options for parents to get access to "better schools" and tutorial services for their kids. They see provisions for parent involvement in drawing up school improvement plans and promises to shake up the status quo. For many, the central issue is how to use the pressure that NCLB puts on schools to make them more effective and more responsive institutions. In fact, pitting educators who see NCLB as an attack against parents who see it as an opportunity is one of the law's major political uses.

This tension is reflected in efforts to advance the privatization agenda in NCLB, which can be seen most clearly in its provisions for school transfers and supplemental tutorial services. (A straightforward voucher program was taken out of the original proposal as part of the legislative compromise that got it passed, though the Administration continues to pursue vouchers through separate means. For example, in the wake of Hurricane Katrina's devastation of schools in New Orleans and surrounding areas, the Administration's "recovery package" earmarked hundreds of millions in public funds for private school tuition.)[11]

NCLB requires schools and districts to spend up to 20% of their federal funds to support transfers out of "failing schools" and to provide "supplemental tutoring" for students who remain in schools "needing improvement." Both the transfer and the tutorial provisions have lots of complications, but the main effects are clear:

- There are nowhere near enough alternative school placements for the growing numbers of students eligible to transfer.[12]
- Private companies are in line to reap the largest share of over $2 billion in earmarked for "supplemental tutorial" providers.[13]
- The funds used to support individual tutorial services and transfers will reduce the sums available for whole school improvement in those same schools.

A key part of this effort to open the public system to privatization involves a special appeal to parents, particularly in poor communities to utilize the law's "choice" and "supplemental tutorial" provisions. In their voucher campaigns, conservatives have learned how to repackage market "reforms" that privatize public services as a form of "parental choice." Similarly, NCLB encourages parents to leave public schools behind and appeals to them as individual consumers of educational services as part of a broader effort to replace local control of institutions like schools with market reforms that substitute commercial relations between customers for democratic relations between citizens.

NCLB, however, does not guarantee parents any new places to go. In districts where some schools are labeled "failing" and some are not, the new law is actually forcing increased class sizes by transferring students without creating new capacity. NCLB does not invest in building new schools in failing districts. It does not make rich suburban districts open their doors to students from poor districts. And it doesn't give poor parents any more control over school bureaucracies than food stamps give them over the supermarkets. The transfer regulations are a "supply-side" fraud designed to manufacture a demand for alternative school placements and ultimately to transfer funds and students to profit-making private school corporations through vouchers.

The link between NCLB's "options for parents" and the Administration's voucher and privatization plans is clearly reflected in the Department of Education's implementation efforts. The DOE has given multi-million dollar grants to pro-voucher groups like the Black Alliance for Educational Options, The Hispanic Council for Reform and Educational Options, and the Greater Educational Opportunities Foundation, to encourage parents to utilize the tutorial and transfer provisions of NCLB. The grants are just another example of how the federal agencies charged with overseeing and improving public education are now run by people intent on dismantling it.[14]

Nevertheless, a portion of the traditional civil rights coalition and a significant sector of popular sentiment in poor communities remain susceptible to the power of NCLB's rhetoric. Nourished by decades of school failure, which has reached desperate levels in urban communities where less than half of black and Latino freshmen typically graduate from high school, some in these communities are understandably less concerned with the looming dangers of privatization than they are with finding ways to use NCLB to pressure schools to make good on their promises to serve all children well. In fact, just how serious the privatization agenda is and how cynically concern for achievement gaps is being manipulated to advance it is currently a major point of difference among those who otherwise share a common interest in addressing issues of educational inequality.

The Education Trust, a Washington, DC-based lobbying and policy organization that was instrumental in designing and passing NCLB, has been particularly active in mobilizing such sentiment. It organized more than one hundred black and Latino school superintendents to denounce opposition to NCLB as an effort to "turn back the clock" and insisted that NCLBs tests and standards are effective and appropriate responses to educational inequality. The Citizens Commission on Civil Rights, another bipartisan lobby, has also supported NCLB's focus on achievement gaps as an important shift in federal education policy. These liberal defenders of NCLB have provided important cover and support for the law.[15]

GROWTH AND LIMITS OF OPPOSITION

The opposition, however, has grown much faster. There are so many things wrong with NCLB – from its grossly inadequate funding, to the obsessive reliance on standardized testing to the punitive political sanctions and the chaotic transfer plans, to the educational malpractice that the law imposes on special-education and bilingual students – that it has drawn increasing opposition from all sides. Forty-seven of 50 states are currently considering legislation challenging some aspect of NCLB. Professional organizations are lining up to pass resolutions calling for major changes when the law comes up for renewal in 2007. Polls indicate that the more people know about the law, the more they oppose it. The National Conference of State Legislatures issued a report calling the law "a flawed, convoluted and unconstitutional education reform initiative that had usurped state and local control of public schools." (NYT 2/24/05) An Illinois school district initiated a lawsuit charging that NCLB's treatment of special education students violated the provisions of another federal law, the Individuals with Disabilties Education Act.[16]

The nation's largest teachers' union, the National Education Association, whose opposition to NCLB earned it a denunciation as "a terrorist organization" by then-Secretary of Education Rod Paige, has filed federal suit against the law, along with eight school districts in Michigan, Texas and Vermont. The suit charges that the law illegally imposes federal mandates and regulations that are not funded, despite explicit language in the law that nothing may "mandate a State or any subdivision thereof to spend any funds or incur any costs not paid for under this Act." The other major teachers' union, the American

Federation of Teachers, has moved from being a strong supporter of the law to being a critic, scrambling to address a groundswell of discontent among its members over NCLB.[17]

Although Democrats have been vocal about the Administration's "broken promises" on funding for NCLB, Congressional leaders from both major parties have conspicuously prevented critics from amending its provisions. Some Democrats have argued that Republican majorities in Congress make re-opening the law risky, fearing it would provide opportunities for privatization and voucher proponents to advance even more aggressive measures. However, growing opposition and the lengthening list of schools stigmatized as "failing" make it certain that reauthorization in 2007 will be a fight.

Already there are numerous reform proposals in formation. They include a moratorium on NCLB's testing mandates, measures to suspend the sanctions in any year that full funding is not provided, proposals to change the testing rules to give schools credit for making relative progress over time, and similar half measures.[18]

What is not yet on the table, however, is an effective national campaign to replace NCLB with a program that can provide desperately needed support for real school improvement strategies, strategies that are not test-driven, not one-size fits all, but that provide a credible basis for tackling the enormously complicated and difficult issues of educational inequality, school accountability, and school improvement. Ultimately it is not enough for opponents to force NCLB off the tracks, because the coming train wreck is, in part, exactly what the free market school crusaders hope to see. As one observer put it, "NCLB is not the answer to a crisis in public education. NCLB is a tool for creating crisis."[19]

The tactical unity of divergent forces currently arrayed against NCLB, the litigation in the courts, and the growing body of reports and commissions documenting NCLB's follies and failures do not yet add up to a movement with the political base, clarity, and clout to move federal policy in a different direction. Part of the problem is the need to change the terms of the debate away from standards and tests and top-down mandates, often misrepresented as "systemic reform," to a focus on teachers and students, and the kind of resources, assessment and accountability systems schools need to build their capacity to serve all children. There also needs to be a shift away from federal and state education policy in service of privatization and market reform, toward a renewed public commitment to schools as local, citizen-run democratic institutions and centers of community life.

Shifting this debate requires explicit recognition of the ways in which, fifty years after legal segregation was outlawed, the dual school system continues to provide a separate and unequal education to students from different racial and class backgrounds, and, especially, of the ways that the standards and testing regime reinforces these divisions instead of reducing them. It also requires that teachers and their unions use their power not just to narrowly defend the system as it now exists, but to advocate for radical reform and urgent expansion of educational opportunity for all children.

To prevent the gaps between educators and parents from being filled by aggressive political campaigns to promote standards, tests, vouchers and privatization, will require effective, sustained public efforts to explain why these "remedies" hold out absolutely no hope of solving the problems of public education or providing real alternatives for those who need them most. Supporters of public schooling need to do a better job of showing how privatization and market reform will do for education what they've done for housing, health care and other sectors of the economy: provide profit-making opportunities for a few well-financed investors and reproduce the class and racial inequalities that exist in the larger society. Finally, building a pro-education coalition requires developing a credible alternative program of reform that combines equity and accountability for all schools, that focuses on the supports needed to improve teaching and learning in classrooms, and that puts school reform in the context of a larger national effort to promote local democratic institutions and reorder social priorities.

NCLB is the culmination of a very active conservative mobilization around schools over several decades. While the "wedge issues" that previously dominated the rightwing education agenda have been eclipsed by larger policy ambitions, they are still there. Using schools to promote military recruitment, school prayer, and even homophobia (a special NCLB provision guarantees the Boy Scouts access to school facilities despite its history of antigay discrimination) are all part of the toxic NCLB mix. A political attack on the independence and objectivity of scientific research is also a central part of the law's "Reading First" provisions, which misrepresent research about the teaching of reading and restrict the use of funds to certain commercial curriculums and instructional packages that favor scripted, test-driven, phonics-based approaches.[20]

Today, federal education policy has become part of a larger political agenda that seeks to erode and privatize the public sector. Though the federal government provides only about eight percent of school funding, the Administration is using federal regulation to drive school policy in conservative directions at the state, district, and school levels. What's changed is not a new federal commitment to "leave no child behind," but the gathering strength of an ideologically-driven political campaign to reform public education out of existence through a strategy of "test and burn." As researcher Gerald Bracey has put it, NCLB "is a weapon of mass destruction targeted at the public schools."[21]

The good news is that the fallout from NCLB is generating a growing resistance at the local, state, and national levels. These efforts prefigure a movement that could, if nourished and deepened, project a vision of a democratic school reform that truly serves both children and society as a whole, and that works to transform public education instead of destroying it. With NCLB making its noxious presence felt in a school district near you, it's a good time to find this resistance and join it.

NOTES

[1] "Senate Approves a Bill to Expand the Federal Role in Public Education," Diana Jean Schemo, *New York Times*, Dec. 19, 2001

[2] Nina Shokraii Rees , Improving Education for Every American Child, Heritage Foundation, February, 1999

[3] See text of NCLB legislation, http://www.ed.gov/policy/elsec/leg/esea02/index.html

[4] Jonathan Kozol, The Shame of America: the restoration of apartheid schooling in America. Pp. 63-64, Crown Publishing: 2005

[5] See "No Child Left Behind: Costs and Benefits," William Mathis, Phi Delta Kappan, May, 2003

[6] Alliance for Excellent Education, Fact sheet on Adolescent Literacy, December, 2004

[7] See Health Insurance Coverage in the United States, 2002, US Census Bureau; 2002 Facts on Child Poverty in America, Children's Defense Fund, & Bureau of Labor Statistics.

[8] Parsing the Achievement Gap, Educational Testing Service, October, 2003

[9] FairTest, Joint Organizational Statement on No Child Left Behind (NCLB) Act, October 2004, http://www.fairtest.org

[10] "26 Conversations About Organizing, School Reform, And No Child Left Behind" Leigh Dingerson Center for Community Change, Chris Brown, Cross City Campaign for School Reform & John M. Beam, National Center for Schools and Communities at Fordham University, April, 2004

[11] Erik W. Robelen and Michelle R. Davis, "Hurricane Aid is on the Way to Districts, Private Schools", January 11, 2006, *Education Week*

[12] See Lori Olszewski and Stephanie Banchero, "Only 1,035 spaces open for city school transfers," *Chicago Tribune*, August 16, 2003; Danny Rose, "The accountability trap: How 'No Child Left Behind' creates crises in public schools," www.onlinejournal.com, August 2, 2003; Alexander Russo, "Slow starts, false starts abound across country," *Catalyst*, September, 2002

[13] "No Child Left Behind: Where Does the Money Go?" Policy Brief by Gerald W. Bracey Education Policy Research Unit (EPRU) Arizona State University, June 2005

[14] "Funding a Movement: Analysis of U.S. Department of Education Grantmaking Reveals Steady Stream of Public Funds to Support School Privatization," People For the American Way, 11/21/2003

[15] See "Don't Turn Back the Clock!" *Education Trust*, November 18, 2003 and "Anaylsis of President George W. Bush's Education Plan," Citizens Commission on Civil Rights, March 1, 2001.

[16] See "NCLB Left Behind: Understanding the Growing Grassroots Rebellion Against a Controversial Law," www.NCLBGrassroots.org, August, 2005; "Opposition to School Law Growing, Poll Says," *Education Week*, April 7, 2004, "Report Faults Bush Initiative on Education," *New York Times*, Feb. 24, 2005, and "Bush Visits School to Speak on Education Law," *New York Times*, January 10, 2006

[17] Plaintiffs In 'No Child Left Behind' Act Lawsuit Will Appeal Decision, press release, National Education Association, Nov. 23, 2005, *NCLB – Let's Get It Right*, American Federation of Teachers, http://www.aft.org/topics/nclb/index.htm

[18] See Legislative Proposals to Amend ESEA/NCLB, http://www.fairtest.org/nattest/Leg_to_ammend_NCLB.html

[19] Danny Rose, "The accountability trap: How 'No Child Left Behind' creates crises in public schools," www.onlinejournal.com, August 2, 2003

[20] See Richard Allington, *Big Brother and the National Reading Curriculum: How Ideology Trumped Evidence*, Heinemen, 2002 and "In Bush administration, policies drive science scholars' group claims" *Education Week*, March 3, 2004, p. 20.

[21] Gerald Bracey, 13th Bracey Report on the Condition of Public Education, *Phi Delta Kappan*, October, 2003

Contributors

BILL ANDERSON has taught in secondary schools in Birmingham, England, for over thirty years. During this period, he was a humanities teacher and was responsible for the pastoral care of older teenage pupils. He has been an active member of the Birmingham Association of the National Union of Teachers throughout his time in teaching, and is currently its full-time deputy general secretary. He is a passionate supporter of comprehensive schools, which his own two children attended. Bill Anderson has also been active within the Socialist Teachers Alliance within the NUT. He serves on the national advisory group of the NUT for secondary education, on the 14-19 working group, and on the influential committee which orders national conference business. He has written a number of articles on the impact of the "modernising agenda" in education and the "remodelling" of the workforce. He is also interested in the role of teacher trades unions in the shaping of education, in the wider union movement and as part of civil society. Email: anderson11a@blueyonder.co.uk

RITA BOUVIER is currently on the administrative staff of the Saskatchewan Teachers' Federation. She has served public education for thirty-one years in varying capacities: as a classroom teacher, as Director of the Saskatchewan Urban Native Teacher Education Program, a sessional lecturer at the University of Saskatchewan, and as a curriculum developer. Rita Bouvier writes in her spare time. Her publications include two books of poetry, *Blueberry Clouds* and *Pâpiyâtak* (released by Thistledown Press in the Spring of 2004 was nominated for Saskatchewan's book of the year) as well as a book co-edited with Angela Ward entitled, *Resting Lightly on Mother Earth*, highlighting educational experiences of Aboriginal people in urban environments. She has been part of a research team examining the experiences of Aboriginal teachers in publicly funded schools in Saskatchewan (*Okiskinahamakewak – Aboriginal Teachers in Saskatchewan's Publicly Funded Schools: Responding to the Flux*) and was part of the Saskatchewan Curriculum and Instructional Leadership Unit's review team of the Northwest Territories (Aboriginal) Teacher Education Program, *Stream to River: Strong Current Teacher Education*. She holds a B.Ed and an M.Ed degree in education from the University of Saskatchewan. Email: bouvierr@stf.sk.ca

VÉRONIQUE BROUILLETTE is an advisor at the Centrale des syndicats du Québec (CSQ), the province's biggest union in the primary and secondary education sector. She deals mainly with issues in tertiary education, on behalf of the CSQ members working as support staff, teachers and professionals in CEGEPs (Québec's general and vocational tertiary colleges) and professionals, support staff and non-tenured professors in universities. She has worked for the CSQ on issues such as higher education in a context of globalization, trends in vocational and technical training, performance plans, public-private partnerships, subcontracting, educational funding, student loans, and school democracy. Véronique Brouillette was a member of a Task Force on higher education and globalization for Education International (EI) an international organization that represents teachers and education workers worldwide. She represented the CSQ at EI's conferences on higher education. Before working at the CSQ, she studied political science and education at Université Laval and taught an Introductory course in Sociology of Education at Algoma University. She has contributed to research projects on the political aspects of education, such as the trend towards decentralization and evaluation as demonstrated in the new managerialism of universities and the creation of school governing boards for primary and secondary schools. Email: brouillette.veronique@csq.qc.net

RAEWYN CONNELL is University Professor at the University of Sydney. A researcher in sociology and other social sciences, she is author, co-author or editor of nineteen books, including *Ruling Class Ruling Culture*, *Making the Difference*, *Gender and Power*, *Schools and Social Justice*, *Masculinities*, *The Men and the Boys*, and most recently *Gender* and the international *Handbook of Studies on Men and Masculinities*. A contributor to research journals across the social sciences, her current research concerns social theory from the point of view of the global south, changing masculinities, neo-liberalism, and intellectuals. Raewyn Connell has been active in movements to reform higher education, in the peace movement, and in several fields of policy around issues of social justice, such as education for disadvantaged children and the role of men and boys in achieving gender equality. In the latter field she assisted a recent United Nations initiative. She has taught in universities in Canada, the United States, Germany and Australia, and tries to use the resources of academic institutions to link researchers and activists internationally. Email: r.connell@edfac.usyd.edu.au.

NATHALIE DUCEUX has taught mathematics in a secondary school in the Seine Saint Denis district, a poor northeast Paris suburb. She was educated at the University of Paris where she obtained a masters degree in pure mathematics. She was involved in the 1980 student movement against the increase of tuition fees. As a teacher she was also active in the Seine Saint Denis parent-teacher movement, which demanded more teachers and financial resources to close the gap with the national average. This movement triggered a wave of teacher struggles against neo-liberal reforms of education during the years that followed, in particular the powerful resistance against the decentralization of education in 2003. For several years, she was a member of the national leadership of France's major secondary school teachers' union, the SNES. She was elected to the national executive where she represented the main left-wing tendency "l'Ecole Emancipée." She has written several articles in the review *L'Ecole Emancipée* and in *Critique Communiste* about the on-going reforms designed to adapt schooling to neoliberal globalisation. She now lives in Thailand. Email: natduceux@yahoo.fr

RICHARD HATCHER is director of research in the Faculty of Education at the University of Central England in Birmingham. He has taught in primary schools and in further education. He has written widely on aspects of education policy with particular reference to social justice issues. Most of his recent publications are critiques of the school education policies of the Labour government: in particular, privatisation and the various forms it takes, but also managerialism in education and issues of social class inequality. Richard Hatcher is an active member of the National Union of Teachers (the largest teachers union in England and Wales) and a member of the executive committee of its Birmingham branch. He is a founder member of the Socialist Teachers Alliance, set up in 1976 and now the principal left grouping within the NUT. He has also been active in the education network of the European Social Forum and in sessions on education at the Forums in Florence (2002), Paris (2003), London 2004) and Athens (2006). Richard has been an invited speaker at numerous education events, both academic and political, including meetings organized by teachers' unions in France and Spain. He is currently involved in campaigns against Academies in Birmingham and nationally as both a researcher and a campaign activist. Email: Richard.Hatcher@uce.ac.uk

KEN JONES is Professor of Education at Keele University, England. He was educated at grammar schools in South Wales and the London suburbs, and at Oxford and Essex Universities. He also learned much from the social and political movements of the 1970s. He taught English at secondary schools in London for fifteen years at a time of teacher militancy and educational innovation and for many of those years was on the national executive of the main teachers' union, the NUT, where he was also active in the Socialist Teachers Alliance. At the end of this period, in 1989, he wrote an analysis of the success of conservatism in curtailing militancy and grassroots innovation – *Right Turn*. Since 1990, working in higher education, he has written about the teaching of English (*English in Urban Classrooms*, with Gunther Kress and others, 2005), about children and television (*Children's Television in Britain* with David Buckingham and others 1999); and most of all about education policy and the conflicts that shape it (*Education in Britain 2003* – a kind of cultural history of post-war schooling). He works with the education network of the European Social Forum. Email: k.w.jones@educ.keele.ac.uk

BRUCE KARLENZIG received Masters' degrees from the University of Saskatchewan in sociology as well as in continuing education. He has been employed at the Saskatchewan Teachers' Federation (STF) since 1994 in a research and policy analysis capacity, with a focus on professional development and equity issues, policies, and programs. Related work has included studies of teachers' workload and work life, teacher certification criteria and processes, equity within the teaching profession, the initial career transition needs of beginning teachers, and the changing roles and responsibilities of the school in addressing equity issues and students' diverse educational and social needs. Prior to his position with the STF, Bruce Karlenzig was employed with the Tripartite Management Unit of the Métis Nation of Saskatchewan (MNS). Research and policy activities carried out in this role concerned Métis self-government goals and issues. Much of this work involved discussions and negotiations among representatives of the Métis, federal, and provincial governments regarding a wide range of partnership (or co-management arrangements) with respect to the design and implementation of various economic initiatives and social programs, including education. His background also includes a number of years of post-secondary teaching experience in various colleges. Email: karlenzb@stf.sk.ca

STAN KARP has been a public school teacher in Paterson, New Jersey for 30 years where he taught English and journalism to high school students and was advisor to award-winning student publications. He was also the lead teacher of the Communications Academy, a small school restructuring project inside his large, comprehensive public high school. He is currently on leave, working for New Jersey's Education Law Center on issues of high school reform. The reforms grew out of the Abbott case, a landmark state court decision that sets the highest standard in the US for funding poor, urban schools. Stan Karp is also an editor of the journal *Rethinking Schools* and has written widely on school reform and educational policy. His articles have appeared in *Education Week*, *Educational Leadership*, and *The National Catholic Reporter*. He is a co-editor of *Funding for Justice: Money, Equity and the Future of Public Education*, *Rethinking Our Classrooms: Teaching for Equity and Justice*, and *Rethinking School Reform: Views from the Classroom*. He was a founding member and past co-chair of the National Coalition of Education Activists, a multiracial network of parents, teachers, and education advocates working for reform and equity in public education. Email: stankarp@aol.com

LARRY KUEHN is Director of Research and Technology at the British Columbia Teachers' Federation and coordinates the BCTF International Solidarity Program. He is a former president of the BCTF and has played an active role in the union for the past 30 years. He is co-author with John Calvert of *Pandora's Box: Corporate Power, Free Trade and Canadian Education*. This 1993 book was one of the first examinations of the potential impact of trade agreements on public education. Over the past dozen years, Kuehn has written many articles for *Our Schools/Our Selves* and other publications tracking the impact of globalization and trade agreements on public education. Larry Kuehn is one of the founding members of the Initiative for Democratic Education in the Americas (IDEA Network), and serves on its coordinating committee. The IDEA Network is a coalition of teacher unions and others concerned about public education throughout the Americas. It has conducted campaigns against the Free Trade Area of the Americas and the General Agreement on Trade in Services (GATS), as well as supported a research network that engages teacher unions in analysis of neo-liberal education policies and develops alternative proposals for more democratic education systems. Email: lkuehn@bctf.ca

GEORGE MARTELL has taught at the Faculty of Education and the Atkinson School of Social Sciences at York University. He was a founder of Point Blank School (an alternative school in Toronto's inner city), a founding editor of *This Magazine Is About Schools* and *Our Schools/Our Selves*, and the author of *The Politics of the Canadian Public School* and *A New Education Politics: Bob Rae's Legacy and the Response of the Ontario Secondary School Teachers' Federation*. An activist in community and parent education politics, George Martell served as an NDP trustee on the City of Toronto Board of Education and then as non-voting chair of the Board's NDP caucus. Later he acted as a senior education policy advisor to the provincial NDP prior to the party winning the 1990 Ontario election and its abandonment of its educational reform project. Since that time he has worked to help bring together Ontario teachers, school-board workers, parents, students and union and community activists into one broad education coalition. He chaired the Ontario Education Alliance and was the research coordinator for the Toronto Education Assembly, out of which the present Campaign for Public Education in Toronto emerged. He is currently working with Toronto's Somali community on educational issues. Email: gmartell@yorku.ca

CAROL ANNE SPREEN is an Assistant Professor in the Department of Education Policy and Leadership at the University of Maryland. Carol Anne's teaching and academic experience is in the field of comparative education and international education policy, with an emphasis on studies of school reform, education rights, curriculum planning and instructional leadership. Her research focuses on equity, diversity, social justice in teaching; curriculum and instructional planning; globalization and educational policy reform/policy borrowing; teachers as agents of change/curriculum-oriented instructional leadership; comprehensive school restructuring and school/community partnerships; comparative multiculturalism/anti-racist teaching; international comparisons of race, ethnicity and identity in schooling. Since 1997 Carol Anne Spreen has been an affiliate of the University of the Witwatersrand and has been actively involved in teacher professional development and policy reforms in South Africa. She holds an MEd from the University of Illinois in Chicago where she was a Chicago public school teacher. She has a PhD from Columbia University in New York, where she developed outreach programs on immigration and identity and helped create an alternative community-service public high school in the South Bronx. Email: spreen@umd.edu

SALIM VALLY has been a social justice activist since high school; in 1976 he was a regional executive member of the South African Students' Movement (SASM). In 1979 he left the country as a result of police repression and studied at York University until 1981. He was also a member of the exile Black Consciousness Movement. In the early eighties he taught at township schools and worked for various adult literacy and progressive research organisations. From 1985 to 1993, he worked as an educator for the Commercial Catering and Allied Workers' Union (CCAWUSA) and later at the COSATU affiliate SACCAWU as the National Educator. During this period he studied part-time at Wits University obtaining his BEd and MEd degrees. Since 1995, Salim Vally has been a lecturer and senior researcher at the Education Policy Unit and the School of Education at Wits University in Johannesburg.He has written numerous articles and co-ordinated various large-scale projects related to education, human rights and social justice issues. These include comprehensive reports on racism in South African Schools; globalization and public education and violence in schools. He coordinates the Education Rights Project, which works with two hundred poor communities and is spokesperson for South Africa's Anti-War Coalition. Email: vallys@epu.wits.ac.za

TEACHER UNION RESEARCH. The authors of *Education and Reform in Southern Cone Countries* from which our report on Latin American education was excerpted are from the Confederation of Education Workers of Argentina, the National Confederation of Education Workers (Brazil), the Teachers College (Chile), and the National Federation of High School Teachers and the Association of Employees of the Universidad del Trabajo (Uruguay). The report was translated by Ruth Leckie and Carmen Miranda-Barrios. Coordination of the teams' work was carried out by the Latin American Observatory on Education Policies of the Laboratory of Public Policies (Rio de Janeiro – Buenos Aires) under the responsibility of Pablo Gentili and Daniel Suárez. Project Assistants were Florencia Stubrin, Julián Gindin and Paola Ferrari. Email for Pablo Gentili: pablo@lpp-uerj.net. The Korean teachers document *Creating Schools with a New Education of Hope* was produced by the School Innovation Team from the Korean Teachers & Education Workers Union. The union can be reached through Lee, Dong-jin. Email: dJl99@hanafos.com

Every kid counts!

BC teachers want to give all students the individual attention they need to succeed at school.

That's why we are calling on the provincial government to live up to its promise to address large class sizes and guarantee support for students with special needs.

A message from the BC Teachers' Federation
For more information, please call (604) 871-2283

EVERY CHILD NEEDS A
TEACHER

The Canadian Teachers' Federation (CTF) and its Member organizations will join Education International and its partners in the Global Campaign for Education (GCE) to promote this year's Global Action Week which will be held April 24-30, 2006 in Canada and around the world.

The theme of this year's campaign is 'Every Child Needs a Teacher' as a means to remind politicians around the world of their promises to achieve Education for All by 2015.

GLOBAL CAMPAIGN FOR
EDUCATION

For ideas on how to take part in this year's campaign, teachers and students can visit the CTF web site at www.ctf-fce.ca.

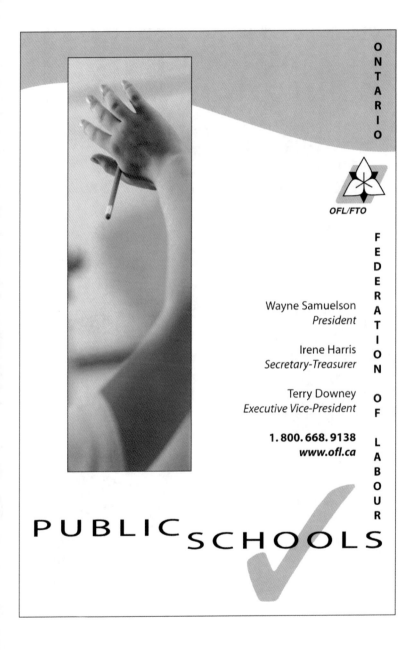

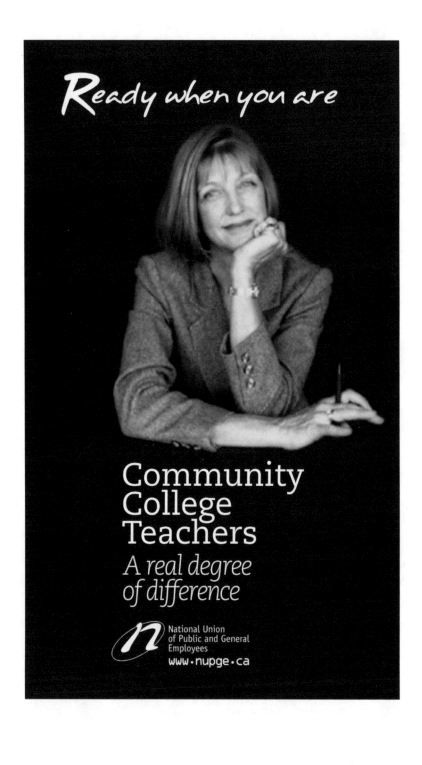

We'll
never stop
fighting
for social justice

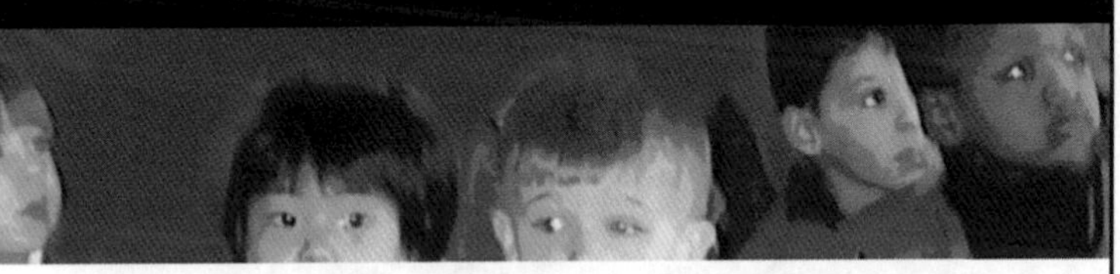

quality child care
no P3s
free tuition

Canadian Union of Postal Workers

www.cupw-sttp.org

Education

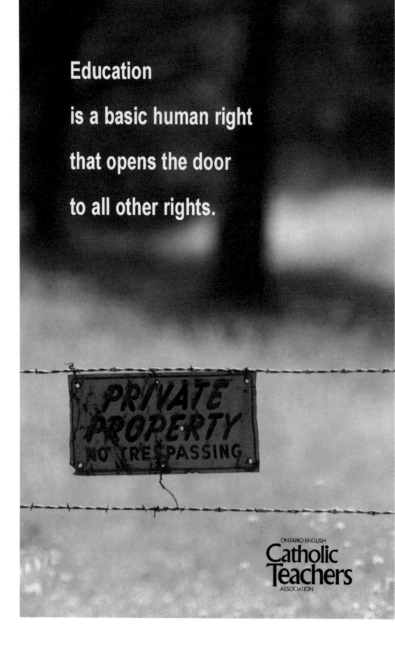

is a basic human right

that opens the door

to all other rights.

ONTARIO ENGLISH
Catholic
Teachers
ASSOCIATION

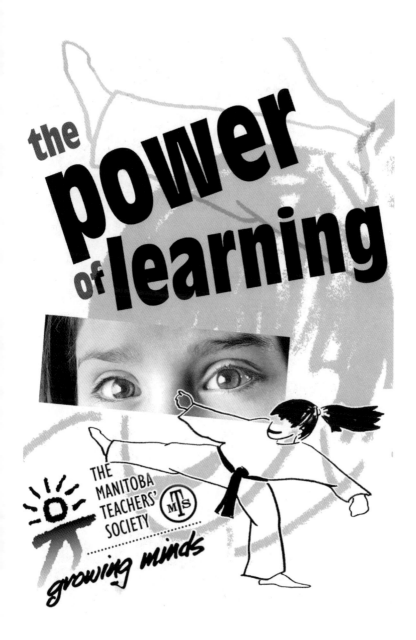

the power of learning

THE MANITOBA TEACHERS' SOCIETY

MTS

growing minds

My work keeps
my community strong
Mary Waddell, CUPE library worker
Canadian Union of Public Employees • cupe.ca
Rebuilding
Strong
Communities

CCPA NATIONAL OFFICE
410-75 Albert St., Ottawa, ON K1P 5E7
tel: 613-563-1341 fax: 613-233-1458
e-mail: ccpa@policyalternatives.ca

CCPA BC OFFICE
1400-207 West Hastings St., Vancouver, BC V6B 1H7
tel: 604-801-5121 fax: 604-801-5122
e-mail: ccpabc@intouch.bc.ca

CCPA MANITOBA OFFICE
309-323 Portage Ave., Winnipeg, MB R3B 2C1
tel: 204-927-3200 fax: 204-927-3201
e-mail: ccpamb@mb.sympatico.ca

CCPA NOVA SCOTIA OFFICE
P.O. Box 8355, Halifax NS, B3K 5M1
tel: 902-430-7461 fax: 902-484-6344
e-mail: ccpans@policyalternatives.ca

CCPA SASKATCHEWAN OFFICE
2717 Wentz Ave., Saskatoon, SK S7K 4B6
tel: 306-978-5308 fax: 306-922-9162
e-mail: ccpask@sasktel.net